THOM WHEELER

THE WAY A RIVER WENT

FOLLOWING THE VOLGA THROUGH THE HEART OF RUSSIA

summersdale

To R. M.

'It is pleasant to have been to a place the way a river went.'

Henry David Thoreau

CONTENTS

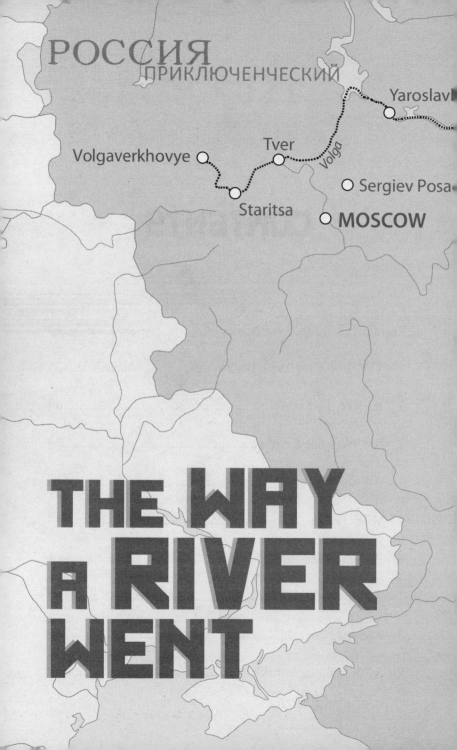

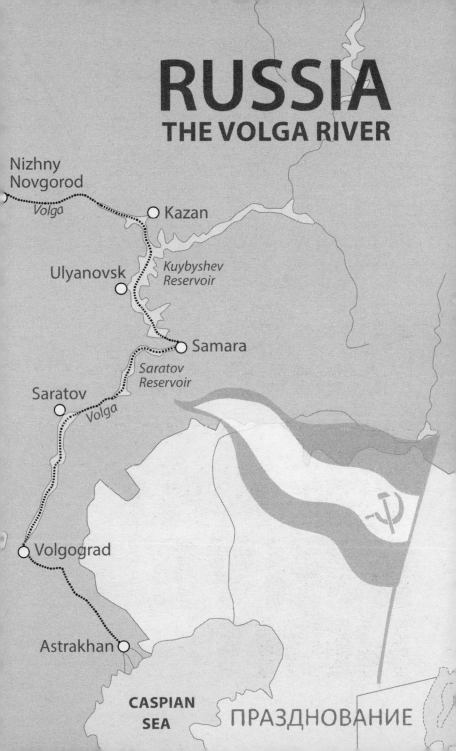

LOVE IN A BIG MUSEUM

I met Vicky Marshall when I was six years old.

Leonid Brezhnev was at the peak of his powers as General Secretary of the Communist Party. I was in the midst of my idyllic and carefree childhood spent tucked away on a small farm in a small hamlet in Dorset with my sister and parents. Along a narrow, stony path that crossed a trickling river before winding through a shady wood of crab apple and hawthorn, our closest neighbours Eric and Edna lived and grew rhubarb. Huge pink and green bundles would appear in our kitchen come the summer, announcing months of crumbles, fools and anything else you could do with a stick of rhubarb. Every year Eric and Edna's granddaughter came to stay with them. Vicky had long blonde hair as straight as uncooked spaghetti and for a while I was in love with her. Or so I thought, but probably more in love with the bike with a crossbar that arrived with her. Hours were spent careering up and down the gravel track on the bike with a crossbar. Her visits were a much anticipated event during those early years at Walnut Farm, until to my complete delight she came to live with her grandparents permanently.

When not at school, our free time was spent enjoying escapades in the great outdoors that surrounded us. The spring and summer months were joyous for us as the adults laboured over the harvest, picnics and home-made wine bringing people together. The barns lent themselves to our fervent imaginations as we spent hours manoeuvring heavy bales to make tunnels and dens, relatively complex structures that allowed us to hide away from the outside world. They survived intact until gradually deconstructed for the needs of cattle and horses with the onset of autumn and then winter.

Whilst we continued to rampage through our blissful childhood, the Cold War was at its height, the Soviet Union powerful and threatening to the outside world yet increasingly rotten on the inside as the Brezhnev years took their toll. By the Moscow Olympics of 1980, Soviet relations with the West were at an all-time low, and one September day that same year our childhood together ended as I was sent off to a new school and Vicky dyed her hair scarlet.

Two words heard nearly as often as Depeche Mode on Radio One during that period were *perestroika* and *glasnost*. They were to define Mikhail Gorbachev's reign as leader of the Politburo and the final days of the Soviet Union. Glasnost was a policy introduced by Gorbachev, who had quickly succeeded Brezhnev's successor Andropov, which called for increased openness and transparency in government institutions and the activities within the Soviet Union. Gorbachev believed it would help reduce the corruption that had raged during the seventies and was still fervent at the highest levels of the Communist Party. Perestroika was a policy of reform that had been proposed by Brezhnev and embraced by Gorbachev, with the ambition of creating a greater awareness of markets and bringing to an end central planning. A policy more than likely very much needed rather than desired after the country had been bled dry by corruption.

I became increasingly interested in the flailing Soviet project whilst Vicky was becoming more interested in things closer to home. Her particular reaction to the safety of her upbringing had kicked in fairly early in her teenage years. To a soundtrack of the Cocteau Twins and Siouxsie and the Banshees she had backcombed her hair and forced her legs into drainpipes before my voice had broken. She had been sent home from a summer camp for sniffing aerosols before J. R. had been shot and 'Relax' T-shirts were a fashion must-have. Well before her fifteenth birthday, I had awkwardly encountered her fumbling around in the back of a steamed-up Ford Escort estate parked up outside the front gate. She was top of her class and good at sport, my best friend that I was proud to have. By the time she was eighteen she had her first proper job as a receptionist at a local firm of solicitors; she wasn't interested in university – she wanted to earn money, rent a flat and buy a car. By adulthood she had expurgated her need to be different and thus marched forward to join the rat race. However, whatever she might have believed and acted upon at the time, she was always destined to be different.

I don't remember seeing very much of Vicky during our twenties: our lives took different paths. Christmas perhaps, and birthdays, but beyond that we would come together very seldom. We had become quite different people with very different outlooks on the world. She had come and gone from a handful of jobs, though she was always in work, always self-reliant and independent. Men came and went, until eventually 'the one' turned up. They got married but it didn't work out and they were acrimoniously divorced within three years. He hadn't been the one after all.

Around the time of Vicky's divorce, I had been putting into action a rather ill-conceived project. I had become a self-styled tour operator, taking people on holiday to Russia. I'd stitched together a handful of tours, ranging from sixteen days crossing the heartland of Siberia to a long weekend in St Petersburg. Having tried them all out myself, I found it inconceivable anybody else wouldn't enjoy them and pay me a substantial amount for their enjoyment. I liked being a tour operator. I just wasn't very good at it.

I had gone into the venture quite unprepared. However, early on it had become clear that I would have to make a small concession to the illusion of professionalism. This took the form of acquiring a licence from the Civil Aviation Authority, the governing body for all things involving fully protected and legit travel to foreign parts.

Anyone who wanted to be considered competent had to be licensed.

The paperwork involved made Australia's immigration procedure appear slapdash. I entered a world of bureaucracy that was frustratingly appropriate for taking trips to Russia. Having taken many days out of my life to project passenger numbers, passenger frequency, passenger humidity, to project income, expenditure, birth rates, death rates, I realised my life had turned into one long projection. Nobody seemed to want any information about stuff I didn't have to project, i.e. the stuff I could actually be sure about and didn't have to predict. However, all my hours spent projecting did eventually land me an interview at the CAA, which in turn led to me getting my hands on a licence.

That turned out to be the easy part. In order to gather together a sufficient number of adventurous travellers to warrant a tour I would need to tap into reserves of charm and persuasion previously unknown to me. I would have to hit the marketplace. My marketing zenith came at the *Daily Telegraph* Adventure Travel Show. I secured use of a tiny space at the trade fair. For the price of a small semi-detached house I could have had an all-singing, all-dancing unit, resplendent with plasma screens, all manner of lighting equipment and a Moccachino-making facility. Much to the annoyance of the voice trying to sell me all these invaluable extras, I stuck to my deeply embedded yet somewhat misguided belief that punters either wanted to go to Russia or they didn't, and that however much caffeine you shoved down their throat, they wouldn't be budged on their decision. Thus I settled for a three foot by four foot cardboard cubicle with no extras, which I decorated with my own photographs.

I spent the first few hours of the show simply wandering up and down the aisles, hypnotised by the colours, sounds and plasma screens of the temporary prefab medina that had been created, and the number of different ways Gore-Tex could be put to use. I was able to rub shoulders (well, to look at) such luminaries of the travel world as Benedict Allen. Jonny Bealby and his team at the Wild Frontiers stand were showing a video of some people riding camels in the desert. I asked him, 'Do you have any trips to Russia?'

'No we don't,' he said.

'Is it somewhere you'd think about going?' I asked.

'Who knows,' he replied before I lost his attention to a lady with a dead animal on her head, who looked like she might actually be able to afford one of his holidays. When I eventually returned to my own stand, encouraged by his words, I quickly realised that I was going to be somewhat overshadowed. Recently uncovered to one side of my cubicle was a Dragoman expedition truck, complete with an army of Drago reps in matching red T-shirts, ready to pounce on any unsuspecting passer-by that showed the slightest bit of interest. And let's be fair, a very big Mercedes truck, custom built to cope with an expedition to pretty much anywhere on the planet, was going to get some interest. Jesus, I was more interested in it than anything I had to offer over at my malnourished stand. Any hostility towards my neighbours was quick to dissolve when I realised that the truck's location could in fact work in my favour, as I would get a steady flow of adventure-seekers passing my stand by default.

As sure as Siberian winters are cold, I was right: it was non-stop all day – okay, most moved swiftly on, having cast a curious glance my way, but at least the stand looked busy. And when anyone did engage further than an initial query I was able to gush forth with facts and figures, tales and trivia, sculpting Russia into the magical destination somewhat far removed from the place I knew it to be. For a brief moment in time I was caught up in the whirlwind of this parallel universe, where dreams can be bought and adventure can be priced up – a place where the power of suggestive imaging reigned supreme! For those few days at the show, I was in the thick of it with the Sundowners and the Imaginative Travellers, and all the other people who had successfully turned adventurous travel into an industry. It was big business now, and there was no place for the little guy with a homemade leaflet and a few blurrily enlarged photographs of indigenous people cuddling cute animals. No, I was out of my depth and went away from the show with the same number of customers I had arrived with: none.

However, it hadn't been a complete waste of time; I had discovered firstly that most of the people already peddling adventure travel tended to wear red T-shirts – which really wasn't my colour. Secondly, I realised that the tours I had put together were in fact pretty good, and if nobody wanted to sign up, then I had stubbornly decided that was their loss. I returned to my office (which was actually a small corner of a garden shed) not the least deflated; if anything, I felt strangely protective of my Russian tours. So I sat and waited for my first client to come knocking, and waited some more... and I continued to wait.

Vicky got wind of my faltering business venture and with a somewhat misguided loyalty went some way to kick-starting things. She booked a four-day trip on my 'Imperial Gems of St Petersburg' tour. She initially did this under a pseudonym which caused me moments of great excitement. I was a little disappointed when I discovered it was Vicky, but quickly saw it as a great opportunity to iron out any teething problems and spend a long weekend with a friend who had become somewhat distant over the years.

Any virgin trip to the Venice of the North will have a visit to the Hermitage high on the list of priorities. With this in mind, the first stop on my Imperial Gems itinerary was Catherine the Great's breathtaking museum. Art has always been political in Russia. Catherine bought her first collection of 225 paintings in 1764 to get one up on Frederick of Prussia, who couldn't afford them due to spending all his money on wars whenever the opportunity arose. She continued getting her hands on national collections from all over – the Campana collection in Italy, the Crozat collection in France, the Walpole collection in England – until she had some four thousand paintings and ten thousand drawings stored at the Hermitage. As fortune would have it, seeing the Hermitage was the only thing, besides plenty of vodka tasting, that Vicky wanted to do, so I had customised the Imperial Gems tour accordingly. Thus armed with cameras and guidebook we passed beneath the giant archway into Palace Square the first morning after our arrival, where we had planned to rendezvous with a certain Dmitry Spiritov.

Dmitry had been born and bred in Odessa, and had spent his childhood in the eighties of perestroika and glasnost, coming of age at the time that the world he had been born into, and groomed to be a part of, was turned on its head. The break-up of the Soviet Union had been a surprise for all the Soviet nations for reasons economic and other, though more of a pleasant surprise for some than for others: Kazakhstan now had full control of its oil, Estonia full control of its tourism.

Whilst others of his generation were hotfooting it abroad to the West, on finishing university in Kiev Dmitry had moved to St Petersburg, seeing no future for himself in the Ukraine. Darwin's theories had never been so true – only the fittest (literally and figuratively) were going to survive the Russia of the nineties. He quickly realised that his survival was going to be dependent on knowing the English language, which he proceeded to learn with an old 'teach yourself' textbook. When others came to the same conclusion he was well positioned to teach them. He opened his first language school in 1995. By 2000 he had two schools and over 2,000 students had passed through his doors.

I had first met Dmitry in 1999 as I trudged the snow-covered January streets of St Petersburg looking for a teaching job. I had started my hunt at the top end of Nevsky Prospect. The first school I went to was located in a poky three-storey building opposite the Alexander Nevsky Monastery, where I was warmly greeted by a confident and handsome Russian. Dmitry was lean and tall with a leading-man presence and chiselled features, complete with a pair of metal-rimmed glasses that he repeatedly bounced on his nose with his hand. Ensconced in Dmitry's office with a warm cup of lemon tea, I learned he had a vacancy and I was just the man for the job. I spent the next eight months working for Dmitry, we became good friends and whilst many of my Russian friends have come and gone over the years, I never lost contact with Dmitry.

It was only ten o'clock but a queue had already developed outside the main entrance to Europe's biggest collection of art. Dmitry considered the collection of backpacks ahead of us before saying, 'I have an idea – follow me.' We followed obediently along the thin gravel pathway that led to the front of the palace, the silvery Neva River rippling under the morning sun only feet away from its turquoise frontage. Into a gloomy courtyard he then led us through a heavy oak-panelled door – 'For servants,' Dmitry pointed out in a conspiratorial tone. We passed into a large airy room that appeared to be a set designer's workshop: half-painted MDF boarding, furniture draped in white sheets, ornate screens fanned randomly about the dimly lit space. Then we followed Dmitry weaving his way between the obstacles, and entered the Hermitage through the back door: Dmitry knew one of the cleaners.

As if passing through the wardrobe into another world we came out into a corridor lined with paintings and tourists, having bypassed the queue and the cash desk. It was at that point I noticed Vicky gazing at Dmitry as if he had just slain a dragon. But Russia was a country in which things happened quickly. Romance was no exception.

The Jordan Staircase's sensual marble, reflected in mirrors fused with the light pouring in from surrounding windows, created the effect of flowing waterfalls. Dmitry took us straight up to the second floor, having made it clear that it would be impossible to see the whole museum that day. It would require several weeks and considerable stamina to see everything. It has been said that to see everything the Hermitage has to offer it would be necessary to walk some nine hundred miles – whether this is true or not, there was certainly much walking to do.

First stop was what used to be called the 'Hidden Treasures Revealed' exhibit, boasting all the paintings taken by the Red Army from private collectors in Germany, after the Second World War – including such luminaries as Monet, Degas, Renoir and Cezanne. Next door to this were several exhibits dedicated to Russian art and culture, icons, ceramics and jewellery from what was called the 'Moscow Baroque' period during the first half of the seventeenth century. Ivory chandeliers, mosaics, tapestries – as we were bombarded by such diverse riches and an admirable commentary from Dmitry, we were caught spinning in a hypnotic historical whirlwind of colour and splendour. If you were going to fall in love anywhere, what better place to do it?

Next was the gobsmacking Malachite Hall with its two tonnes of impressive malachite columns, boxes, bowls and urns. Then into a concert hall once used for small balls – complete with an eighteenth-century silver tomb containing the remains of Alexander Nevsky. Hall followed sumptuous hall: the Nicholas Hall, the Fore Hall, the Field Marshal's Hall, Peter the Great's Hall, the Armorial Hall dazzlingly bright with its display of silver. The 1812 Gallery followed, with portraits of Russian and Napoleonic war leaders, and the Hall of St George. And on it went, into the Little Hermitage and the Pavilion Hall, a sparkling room of white and gold, chandeliers, tables and columns, the windows of which looked out onto Catherine the Great's hanging garden, the floor mosaic beneath them copied from a Roman bath. A marble, malachite and glass triumphal arch announced the beginning of the Italian section and, fortunately for Vicky and my weary legs, that it was also time for lunch.

As we crossed the Palace Square, Dmitry and Vicky walked some paces behind: they only had eyes for one another. The sumptuous majesty of St Petersburg's number one imperial gem had worked its magic. Vicky and Dmitry had walked into the Winter Palace several hours earlier as singletons travelling life's path alone. After journeying through several centuries of Russian history together, they had stepped back out onto Palace Square in love.

Two years and three months later I received an invitation to their wedding.

CHAPTER ONE

THE SOURCE (OR LITTLE BEGINNING)

*'Every country has its national river and Russia has the Volga –
the longest river in Europe, the queen of rivers – and I was one
of the many who went to bow to her majesty River Volga.'*
Alexandre Dumas

My face was distorted as if looking into a fairground mirror. I was completely hypnotised by my reflection. I was unblemished, my face stretched free from lines, bobbing about in this pool of water. I moved my head back, perfectly framing my reflection within the square woodwork of the well. Stepping further away, my mutant other self broke up into fragments that soon faded like bubbles released into the sky. I stared down at the Source.

I was delivered from my trance when a bulky babushka bounced me to one side. She began lowering a bucket with one arm and crossing herself furiously with the other. The chapel we were in had been built up around the source like a Finnish sauna. It had the same smell – the same damp air and slat benches around the outside – only there were clusters of burning candles and icons decorating the walls, austere piety keeping watch on all who entered. Once alone, I did as the old lady had done, lowered one of the buckets and sipped the cold water in hope of purification... and waited.

Back in the open air under the warm sun I stood on a small arched bridge festooned with garlands and followed the progress of the narrow, crystal-clear stream as it set off on its gargantuan journey through the heart of Russia. A gentle breeze caught the lush grass of the surrounding pastures whilst crows squawked nearby. I passed a small kiosk where a man sold plastic water containers and bottles; there was an impatient queue outside – the purification business was good. Back at the taxi, I collected my pack and paid the driver his small fare, and he took his leave with the same bemused look that he'd offered earlier. Some persuasion had been required to acquire his services, the driver remaining convinced my valuable time would be better spent visiting the local monastery.

Ten, fifty, one hundred metres away from the source, and with the growing distance came peace. I left behind the hubbub of the birds and the muffled chatter of the water gatherers. A wind tickled the beech trees and willows that shaded the embryonic river from the rising sun, as the Volga curled tightly like a coiled spring before release. Soon the shimmering trickles would be launched into the youthful river. I sat down in the reedy grass that followed the riverbank loyally. I wanted to hold onto that moment of birth just a little longer – this stage of the river's journey where the Volga was still seemingly untouched by the world that it had so greatly impacted on. The clear icy water was like a magnifying glass on the rocks and plants of the riverbed.

Thirty kilometres from the source – or the *Etochnik*, which translates as the 'little beginning' – was Volgaverkhovye, a small village where I had arranged to meet my Man Friday. This particular Man Friday, when he wasn't organising boat trips, horse treks, home stays or just about anything else a tourist to the region could require, purveyed river-going vessels over the internet. It was with one such vessel that I intended to travel the 180 kilometres down river to the town of Tver on the first leg of my journey to Astrakhan for Dmitry and Vicky's wedding. I was taking the scenic route along the river, the imminent celebration having given me the opportunity to make a journey I'd been harbouring thoughts of for some time. I had just under two months to reach the church on time for the July ceremony. I planned to boat along what was widely considered to be the most manageable part of the Volga before it abruptly mutates into the behemoth waterway of Stalin's industrial vision. Leaving the boat in Tver I would follow the course of the river beyond Moscow and then south towards the sea, travelling by bus, train and any other appropriate conveyance. My contact went by the name Captain Pasha and had reassured me, 'I think no problems with making your wish.' True to his words he had sent me pictures of a water-going craft, which appeared to perfectly match my requirements. With a head full of romantic images of lavender, cow parsley and wooden boats floating through a bygone Russia, I had been quick to snap up my new boat.

The Russians refer to their great river as Mother Volga, a waterway that flows through the heart of Western Russia, from north of the capital Moscow south to its delta and into the Caspian Sea. It meanders some two thousand miles – sources state between 2,293 and 2,589. For centuries the river has been feeding the people of Russia both physically and metaphysically, a source of legend, myth and spiritual strength as well as food. One better-known myth speaks of two sisters, Volga and Vazuza. They argued about who was cleverer and thus deserved the happier life. One day Volga suggested they stop arguing and simply leave home and get on with their lives; that way they would see who was better and with the passing of time all their arguments would find resolution. So competitive was Vazuza that in order to get a head start she left during the night. However, she wasn't fast enough even with this advantage, and the next day Volga caught up with her. Seeing that Volga was the fastest, Vazuza lost her stomach for the fight and decided to concede, and seeing that her sister was heading that way anyway asked her for a ride to the Caspian Sea. Volga, being a kind-hearted sort of girl and still smugly basking in her victory, happily gave her defeated sister a ride, and has been doing so ever since, Vazuza being a tributary of the Volga.

THREE VOLGA FACTS

- The river is so wide in places that it's impossible to see from one side to the other.
- The western bank of the river is what is called a high bluff, occasionally reaching up to 60 feet above the river level.
- The river went by several different names, including Atil, Itil and Idil, until eventually Volga was settled on.

I started to walk again. The river morphed into adolescence before my very eyes as if in a time-lapse video. The newborn I'd spent joyful moments with only hours earlier was beginning to grow in stature, getting wider and stronger. Foam began to appear as currents grew in strength and clashed beneath the surface. Rather than jumping across from one side to the other I was now stuck on the north bank. The speed of the current picked up as the river evolved; the slimy rocks that had poked their sharp pointed heads above the surface earlier were now submerged beneath several feet of water.

Tracks running down to the water's edge provided the first indicator that I was close to the village. Lanky blades of grass had been flattened. I followed one of the tracks away from the river. In the distance was a shabby wooden-slat house, faded turquoise paintwork clashing with the lush green surrounds, no other buildings in sight. The area around the house was shambolic: upturned dinghies lay as if abandoned after a shipwreck, whilst patched-up tarpaulin hung from the sides of the house, sheltering broken bits of furniture. Three barrel-bellied ponies munched on grass nearby, the momentum of each bite steadily moving them forward in slow motion. I made my way around the obstacles in search of a door to knock on. The face of a girl appeared at a dusty window on the first floor. She ran down and peered from behind the frame of an open doorway.

'Where is Volgaverkhovye?' I asked, thinking that perhaps she was the only survivor after the 'Massacre of Volgaverkhovye'. The girl giggled before vanishing out of view. In seconds she was standing beside me.

'This is Volgaverkhovye,' she was quick to tell me with an expression of glee. Looking around I could see no other buildings in any direction, no other buildings that might have been making a valued contribution to Volgaverkhovye's status as a village. The spindly girl, rather awkward in her body but apparently comfortable in my company, continued in English.

'You are here to meet the captain, yes?' I nodded confirmation. 'Tea?'

I followed her around the back of the house where she signalled for me to sit on a weather-beaten bench offering a panoramic vista out over scrubland to a line of trees on the horizon. An occasional car could be seen bobbing along the unsealed road I had travelled along to the source only hours before. A large bearded man with round spectacles soon arrived. He greeted me with a loud throaty belch before joining me on the bench, and introducing himself as Pasha. His salutation had the girl laughing hysterically. Pasha followed up his introduction with a more traditional hand to shake.

'So you want to boat on the river.' He roared before scratching his chin in consideration. 'I have a boat for you...

and she is vary vary buteful!' he exclaimed with a tone suggesting he was pimping out a person and not selling me an old clinker-built dinghy. 'I will take you to her and you will get to know each other... a courtship.' Perhaps there had indeed been some confusion and all talk about boats had been code for something else. 'You will stay with us tonight and then we will say goodbye to you and the boat in the morning.' The captain was no-nonsense – he had it all worked out... or so I thought.

**

Pasha's dacha was intimate and could have been the below deck of a seventeenth-century galleon; there wasn't a right angle to be seen. Ceilings were low, the naked wooden floorboards mostly loose and often warped. To call it cluttered would be an understatement. Perhaps an estate agent would have called it 'homely'. I was given a room on the south side of the building which offered the same view as I had had from the bench. It was a dorm-style space with two sets of bunk beds and was littered with the debris of travellers past. Worn and heavily dog-eared books in English lay abandoned, items of clothing inhabited a wardrobe that languished on a lean. An ashtray sat brimming over with stale butts, empty beer bottles made a fairly good stab at being a work of modern art – either that or a very good advert for Baltika. The window was free of glass; instead, more of the hessian I'd seen on the front door was rolled up to one side in way of a blind. A makeshift coffee table (a crate and a slice of MDF) was adorned with unwashed coffee cups, stained brown sugar and caked teaspoons. I didn't have much time to soak up the atmosphere, as Pasha had quickly rallied. Shaslyk, a form of shish kebab, could already be smelt sizzling on an open fire at the front of the building.

I learnt as the evening progressed that Pasha was a master of irony, possessing a deep-rooted perverse take on the world he had found himself a part of. I quickly learnt to take much of what he said with a splash of *smetana*. He claimed to be of Viking ancestry and considering the man and the environment I'd found him in I couldn't dispute this. His bushy ruddy beard helped, slightly offset by the need to push his thin metal-rimmed spectacles back up his nose every time he poked a piece of meat. He was quite the host, ably assisted by his daughter Zhenya. Mrs Pasha was away in Moscow, which left me more than a little curious as to the woman behind the colossus of a man. Despite appearances Pasha was also quite the businessman – he had already sold me an unseen river-going craft for five hundred quid.

If I'm honest, this was less a result of his business acumen and more a result of my enthusiasm. I'd bought it over the internet sight unseen, driven to part with my cash by daydreams. I had been putty in his virtual hands. So far, though, the gamble was paying off. Having seen the vessel, I was wholly satisfied with my purchase, and judging by Pasha's generous and friendly welcome he was obviously satisfied with the five hundred quid he had received for a boat that was certainly in the autumn of its life, if not fast heading towards the winter. It was a thirteen-foot dinghy the shape of a desert boot, with space and seating enough for two fully grown adults. The deal was made sweeter for me by Pasha agreeing to buy the boat back once I'd finished with it.

Despite Pasha's being in receipt of the equivalent of three months' salary for him, the evening was punctuated by his attempts to sell me 'add-ons', questionable sea-going items he just happened upon lying around the house. The first piece to appear for auction was a compass. After Pasha had finished extolling its virtues I was left convinced that I needed such an item for my forthcoming voyage – until, in a moment of clarity and in the nick of time, it dawned on me that the first 300 kilometres of the linear Volga River was the last place I would require such a navigational instrument. He then happened upon what can only be described as an antique esky or cool box. Pasha started with a 5,000-rouble price tag. I was more concerned by its water tightness than its dubious value, thanks to the glaring gash down the side. He did concur that it would require a degree of maintenance; I concurred that it would make a good addition to the fire. He moved on to exhibit three.

His pitch was full of relish as he tried to sell me a rudder. What I didn't know was that until a short while ago the rudder had belonged to the boat I'd recently bought from him for five hundred quid! As I was blissfully ignorant that my new acquisition was now without one, my lack of interest prompted him to move on to a set of matching life jackets, which looked as if they had been on board the *Titanic* or at least a Russian ship of the same generation, sinking at the same point in history. Disarmed by my host's fervour at this point, I quite happily parted with 1,000 roubles for the pair of buoyancy aids that might one day save my life.

Pasha, very happy with the sale, broke open another bottle of cheap Russian vodka.

Pasha and his wife, up until the mid-noughties, had been Muscovites through and through, living the Russian big-city dream, ducking and diving, wheeling and scheming – small fish in a big pond. Then one day – literally one fine morning, according to Pasha – he woke from a heavy slumber and decided enough was enough. His bread and butter had been running a little street-side kiosk; his earnings were okay but nothing in comparison to the 'biznizmen' who knocked on his wooden door every month gently requesting their share of the profits, which according to Pasha (after a few slugs of vodka) was not inconsiderable. His predicament was made even worse by a change in Russian law that outlawed street-side trading. This change was enforced with an iron fist, and virtually overnight the colourful, not to say very convenient world of the kiosk vanished in Russia's larger cities. With four very nearly teenage daughters, Pasha decided it was time to get out; he had a dacha and some land not far from Moscow, he had a solid grasp of English and it was time to 'enjoy the fruit of tourism'.

Pasha packed his daughter off to bed and led me outside into the now cool night. We sat looking out upon the darkness that covered provincial Russia, with the faint sound of the river just audible nearby.

'This is all I need now,' said Pasha with an air of resignation. 'Russia is broken, perhaps it always has been.' I knew where Pasha was going with this. I'd heard it before from other Russian friends, all doom and gloom, a fatalist view of their lot which went some way to burying a deep pride in their country. I bid goodnight to Pasha whose closing words were: 'Tomorrow I will show you something.' I couldn't wait.

***

The planned one night at Pasha's dacha turned into three days and three nights. The following morning over breakfast he suggested I join him and his daughter Zhenya for a trip out in the horse and cart. The only clue as to where we would be going was proffered by Zhenya: 'To see a fairytale.' Like the river that flowed past her home, Zhenya was still young and still beautifully untainted by the world around her.

Travel by horse and cart, without the noise of an engine, left room for the delightful sounds of the countryside to wash over our senses: birdsong and a light breeze rustling through trees, the clip-clop-clip of the horse's heavy feet hitting the hard black soil. Unruly fetlocks bounced up and down with each pace as the weary barouche creaked and groaned its way forward, bending and flexing in compliance with the uneven terrain. We lurched along across worn-out farmland, neglected scrubland, through wooded copse offering brief respite from the growing heat of the sun. Pasha nonchalantly guided Boris the cart horse, casually holding the reins of the huge metal snaffle that sat tight against the corners of Boris' now frothy mouth. Every now and again the horse would throw his head back in the air, sometimes as if to say, 'This is fun, let's not stop yet,' and other times to say, 'Yeah, alright boss, not so hard with the hands!'

During our journey out neither Pasha nor Zhenya said very much. They appeared to be letting the surroundings control the mood and do their talking for them as they soaked up the Russian heartland with pride, both oozing contentment. It was apparent there was nowhere else in the world they would rather be. After a couple of hours it was Zhenya who broke the hypnotic sounds of the countryside: 'Not far now, over the next hill and we're there.' I still had no idea where 'there' was but was enjoying the element of surprise and grateful to my hosts for giving it to me. Eventually Pasha heaved the cart to a standstill on the edge of an evergreen forest. He climbed down to the ground, gesturing that we should follow. We had stopped at the end of a waterlogged track.

'Impossible to carry on with the cart, but it is not far to walk and Boris will be happy for a rest,' Zhenya proffered. For the first time I noticed that if a dog looks like its owner then by the same rule Boris was most definitely the equine version of Pasha. They both possessed long heads attached to thick muscular necks, with eyes that suggested nothing would surprise them.

We trudged along the muddy track deeper into the woods, where whole areas of trees had been felled but there appeared no pattern or method in the cutting. Was it woodland alopecia – surely man would have been more methodical in his approach to cutting down the forest?

'No, this is man,' replied Pasha. 'They take the ones they can easily get to – nobody is thinking about what it looks like to you... or me.'

Some two hundred metres further on and there it was: my companions glanced in my direction, allowing the sight to sink in, observing my reaction. Initially I thought I was looking at a wealthy Muscovite's country dacha in mid-build. A two-storey wooden mansion set in the middle of the forest – what a wonderful place to spend those long summer weekends. Then after a further few moments it dawned on me that I was looking at a mansion in something beyond the mid-stage of deconstruction.

Pasha couldn't contain himself any longer. 'The house was probably built by the industrialist called Markov at the end of the nineteenth century. It was his suburban dacha. However, there are now many theories on its origins.' He paused to build up the suspense before continuing. 'Another story tells that a builder from St Petersburg called Sazonov built it for his second wife.'

To one side of the house's shell stood a tower with a decorative balcony about two feet wide skirting its perimeter. Pasha saw me looking over at it.

'The tower is said to match a published draft produced by the famous architect called Ropet. However, it is not known if Ropet was the architect himself or his ideas were taken by somebody else.' Pasha had turned into tour guide, yet despite his efforts it was safe to say nobody really had a clue about the house and its history. The tower was indeed spectacular, though. I thought it was quite Mongol in its cylindrical design, sharp and angular, coming to a point like a wizard's hat. Timber stabilisers poked into each of the corners.

The time-weary main house had an intricate gable carved in shapes like stick people joined together as in a paper necklace. We clambered over rotting timbers that blocked the main entrance. Pasha followed at my shoulder; he had been to this place many times before but appeared to still be intrigued by it.

'In the past, people have found all sorts inside – posters, propaganda literature... Somebody found in the attic a newspaper that dated back to 1891. But there is nothing here now.' He kicked a piece of wood as if to emphasise his point. Unhinged and discarded doors leant against the only bare stone wall in the building. We stumbled over half-burnt picture frames and plastic crates, rotting beams and joists that had crashed down from above.

Making sure Zhenya hadn't followed us in, Pasha was clearly very excited to tell me about a man who had made the abandoned house his home in the seventies.

'He was here for maybe three years. At first he would go into Staritsa looking for work, usually in the summer, then over time he was seen less and less until eventually he was found here by children... he was dead.' Pasha paused to get my full attention before finishing his gloomy anecdote. 'Drink... he drunk himself to death.'

The mansion we were standing in was a perfect metaphor for Russia as a whole – a country that had been and continued to be abandoned, leaving an unstable shell. Stalin had once wiped out a generation of the dynamic; Putin with his self-promoting policies had furthered the decline. Many Russians simply left the countryside, heading for Moscow, Petersburg, London, Paris, Berlin – why rot in the provinces? It happens the world over yet perhaps this migration is simply starker in Russia because of the gaps it has left in the economy. Maybe it was only a matter of time before Russia's cross-beams and joists came crashing down as well, held up by an increasingly rotten leadership.

That evening we were joined for dinner by Pasha's neighbours, Feodor and Gemma Dukovski. Feodor possessed a sculpted beard that would have made Lenin a little envious. His wife, not surprisingly with such a name, wasn't Russian at all. Gemma Dukovski had grown up in a small village in the Cotswolds before heading off to university to study Russian, after which she took a job with a law firm in Moscow. It was during this period she met and fell in love with Feodor, whom she soon married. Three years after giving up her job and moving back to Feodor's country home, she was expecting their first child and judging by her shape very soon indeed. The imminent arrival wasn't going to stop Feodor, however, who landed his intent to drink onto the garden table in the form of a bottle of vodka.

'This not shite,' he said, as if reassurance was required. That was the only English I heard him speak all evening.

Gemma spoke to me of life in Moscow, which I asked if she missed.

'Sometimes,' she mused, and I couldn't help thinking that perhaps she did more than she was letting on.

Pasha held forth for most of the evening with funny stories punctuated by jokes, declarations of love for the assembled group and declarations of hate for various others. Somewhat inevitably, the evening descended into Pasha ranting about the state of Russia, and in no uncertain terms advising Feodor and Gemma to 'get your unborn child away from Russia'. Something neither of them had the slightest intention of doing – even if there had been enough time. Their child would be born in the Russian heartland and would grow up as a Russian, albeit a Russian with more than a passing interest in the weather forecast.

***

The time eventually arrived for me to cement my relationship with *Molly*, my new rowing boat, the name having been suggested by Gemma for reasons that remained undisclosed. Pasha pushed us away from the jetty just as the sun was getting up some heat. Zhenya was joining me for the first leg down to Staritsa, where Pasha would meet us having dealt with some 'business' in the town. There was a strong possibility his activity would amount to little more than simply buying potatoes but I wasn't going to spoil the air of intrigue he obviously enjoyed creating.

Water gently splashed over the bow of the boat as Pasha vanished out of sight. I felt elated, having daydreamed about doing this exact same thing many times in the prior months – rowing down the Volga, surrounded on either side by the sleepy and soothing Russia of bygone days. Passing the golden domes of churches that would have been standing for hundreds of years. Fishermen perched on the banks, their rods more prop than tool. Children played in the shimmering water, throwing balls to one another, trying to drag their friends under. The current carried us towards Staritsa. The Volga was now coming of age and was taking me with it.

After nearly three hours we rounded a bend and there in the distance the river lapped the muddy bank in the shadow of the ochre-tinged walls of Staritsa's Monastery of the

Assumption. I had found my rhythm and had managed to keep the oars in the horseshoe rowlocks for at least twenty minutes without one or both of them bouncing out. We passed under an iron bridge that spliced the two halves of Staritsa together. According to Zhenya it would be the second to last bridge I'd see across the Volga. A passer-by, who had stopped to watch us disembarking, gestured up at the bridge: 'Great place for the bungee jumping.' Then pointing at *Molly* said, 'Good luck with your journey. It's a long way yet.' He laughed and continued on his way.

Zhenya led me up the winding gravel lane past the freshly painted monastery. We were soon within the heart of one of Russia oldest towns. Staritsa was established in 1297 under its original name of Gorodok, meaning 'small town'. In 1365 the settlement moved to the lower left bank of the river and was renamed Novy Gorodok, meaning 'new small town'. In the fifteenth century the name was again changed, this time to Staritsa meaning 'former river bed'. Should it move again, history suggests it will be renamed Novy Staritsa or New Former River Bed. Heraldists misrepresented the name of the town and put an aged nun on the coat of arms, this being another meaning of the Russian word *Staritsa* – according to Pasha, anyway.

Vladimir of Staritsa had been the last Russian prince in line to the throne. He was Ivan the Terrible's cousin and their often complicated relationship was featured in Sergei Eisenstein's film *Ivan the Terrible*. After a childhood in Moscow, Vladimir moved out to Staritsa where he married and lived in peace until 1553 when Ivan the Czar fell ill. Most of the boyars (noblemen) prudently refused to swear allegiance to Ivan's baby son; instead they wanted to put on the throne his cousin Vladimir, who although not the greatest choice of leader could hold more than a gaga conversation and wasn't prone to dribbling – well, not as much. As it happened, Ivan recovered and became something of a changed man. He persuaded Vladimir to return to Moscow and have no contact with his disloyal boyars; he made Vladimir agree to being regent to the baby son in the event of his death. But with the start of *oprichnina*, the fickle Ivan once again saw his cousin as a threat.

QUICK ASIDE ABOUT *OPRICHNINA*

Oprichnina was the period of Russian history between 1565 and 1572 during which time Ivan the Terrible instituted a domestic policy of repression, secret police, public executions and the confiscation of land from the aristocracy. His policy, intended to secure ultimate power, was enforced by the political police who went by the name of *oprichniki*. The name comes from the Russian word *oprich*, which means 'apart from' – very apt for the relationship between the despotic Ivan and his subjugated people. The contemporary writer Vladimir Sorokin's book *Day of the Oprichnik* (2006) depicts a Moscow in the year 2028, blending futuristic technology with the draconian codes of Ivan the Terrible (not entirely unlike Moscow in the present day).

In 1569, Vladimir and his family were accused of high treason and forced to take poison. This precipitated the extinction of the Rurik dynasty and the advent of the Times of Troubles from 1598 to 1613, during which period a famine killed one third of the population, adding somewhat to the already troubled times.

Along the dusty main road through Staritsa, popular with articulated trucks, we walked past the crumbling stonework of the Illyskaya Church and aging limestone houses, which made up much of the town. Zhenya left me at the bus station to go and meet her father, the both of whom I'd meet later back at the river. Young mothers struggled with prams up the steps through the heavy iron doors of the station. Come to think about it, just about everyone in Staritsa seemed to have a pram. Even some of the young men who appeared not to have slept for many years were pushing prams. And there were a lot of kids under the age of three, whose presence went some way to contradict reports of Russia's dying population. I wondered if Putin had offered some sort of incentive to reproduce in order to counter the diminishing numbers. Those not pushing prams were either driving taxis or just hurrying around appearing to be busy doing something – as is the Russian way. Can there really be so many urgent things for everyone to do? It was a relief to see a couple of squatters chewing sunflower seeds on the street, simply and unashamedly wasting time.

It wasn't long before I became aware of a man sitting at the table next to mine in the station cafe. He had a pram parked up, but in place of any living breathing baby there was a big plastic bag full of sugar. I noticed him because he was staring at me with an expression that suggested I had offended him in some way. When our eyes met, I was taken by how pale he was and how skeletal his features were.

His fingers pushed an unlit cigarette around the table top, weaving it between small pools of spilt coffee. In an attempt to dispel some of the increasing discomfort I was feeling, and aware that if indeed this man was as menacing as he looked I was probably close enough to *Molly* to make a successful getaway, I introduced myself. He simply nodded very slowly as if to suggest he already knew who I was. More likely he already knew that he was making me very uncomfortable. Moments later he simply said, 'You want Krokodil.'

I had heard of Krokodil, 'the drug that eats junkies', but knew very little about it. Russia has more heroin users than any other country in the world, up to two million according to unofficial estimates. There are efforts to stem the flow of Afghan heroin into Russia but with limited success, and the street price goes up and up; thus addicts who can't afford the next hit, unsurprisingly, have turned to something else. Desomorphine, or 'Krokodil' as it is known on the street, is a synthetic opiate considerably more powerful than heroin. It has been given its nickname because its effects quickly turn the skin scaly like that of a crocodile.

My answer to his question was 'No, thank you,' and by then I wasn't sure about tea and cake either. I decided it was probably time to leave before I found myself out of my depth even on dry land. As my neighbour watched me gathering myself in readiness to depart, he pulled back the hood that had shaded his face and started chuckling, as if now he had revealed his whole face to me we could in fact be friends.

'Let me show you my town?' He spoke with a voice borrowed from Darth Vader. I wasn't sure how a refusal to the offer would play itself out. I found myself glancing down at my wrist... I had no watch so that wasn't going to help my excuse. I said that I had to leave, which I did to the echoes of his throaty laughter.

***

I rejoined Pasha and Zhenya back down by the river. I had enjoyed Zhenya's company on this first leg in *Molly* and over the previous days, so was sorry to be leaving her. Zhenya's candour had gone some way to counter the often dispiriting reality existing beyond the river bank in provincial Russia. Her intrinsic hopefulness had been contagious and in turn given me much hope for my journey and the country I would be travelling through. Pasha I would see again when he collected *Molly* in a few days' time downriver in Tver, but when Zhenya stepped forward with an outstretched hand to shake in way of a goodbye, I felt a little stab of sadness. Pasha and his family's warm hospitality wasn't over just yet – as it had been arranged for me to meet his brother who lived further along the river in Tver, my next destination.

I continued downriver as the fluffy white clouds of the past few days were replaced with dark menacing cumulonimbi, which created a suitable atmosphere for the river's transformation into adulthood. Very soon the water grew darker and the rocky riverbed less visible, which suggested the depth was increasing. There was litter by the water's edge, remnants of intemperance: cans, cigarette butts, even syringes. It felt like the purity of the *Etochnik* was fading, to be replaced by something adulterated and dirty.

I planned to cover the 80 kilometres to Tver in two days, maybe less. That first night I had a vision of what would await me...

A hearty meal with some locals, perhaps freshly caught fish cooked riverside, with some seasonal vegetables freshly cooked, washed down with a few glasses of vodka and followed by some raucous riverside dancing. I would then spend the night beneath the stars by the Volga in my paper-thin four-seasons sleeping bag, listening to the water splash the bank with the sounds of the night providing gentle comfort.

That didn't happen... but before that disappointment I first discovered how difficult it was to row for extended periods of time. At regular intervals I had to down oars and glide for a while to give my arms a rest. I had rowed in the past but never more than a gentle maritime equivalent of a saunter. Unlike much of the early stages of the Danube (of which I had some experience – walking along the footpath and not rowing), with its riverbanks perfectly manicured and boasting regular picnic spots for walkers and cyclists, the Volga even in the early stages has no concessions to leisure activities. It is a working river and not one, it would seem, to be enjoyed aesthetically.

MY BRIEF EXPERIENCE WITH THE DANUBE

It was a few years earlier that I had bought a flight for ten pence and travelled by aeroplane to Munich. I did this for two reasons: firstly the ticket was ten pence and thus impossible to ignore (okay, after tax a little more, but still cheap). Secondly I'd been having dreams: dreams about water, dreams about rivers. These nightly episodes coincided with my reading of a book, a tale of Victorian pioneering gusto about a man risking life and limb to travel up the Lena River in Siberia, a questionable pursuit and one that caused the protagonist many an hour of heartache and torture at the hands of vodka-soaked locals and haemoglobin-guzzling mosquitos.

This particular blend of derring-do and apparent masochism roused in me a brief period of reflection, one I decided I would have to act upon. I reached the conclusion that what my life needed was a challenge. Just hearing the word sent a shiver down my spine. The 'from A to B in the fastest time possible' sort of challenge, the 'if you don't make your target you've failed' sort of challenge. I had somehow developed quite a talent for justifying failure. What other people would call failure I would call a change of plan. It was time to awaken my inner competitor.

I had no intention of following in the footsteps of the aforementioned author – too dangerous – but my dreams were suggesting that my challenge should also involve a river, and of course there were plenty more rivers in the world that would be far more hospitable and easier to navigate.

Those who tend to shy away from challenges are seldom ready for a challenge when it comes along. I think my mother might have said that. She was right.

A month before I flew to Munich all I knew about the Danube was that it was the river that split the beautiful city of Budapest in Hungary, that and the song 'Blue Danube' had obviously been written with the river in mind. Having done the minimal amount of research, I was able to discover that the Danube was a pretty long river, joining the Black Sea several thousand kilometres away in Romania, its source in the forest not far from the Bavarian town of Ulm.

I began my walk in Ulm, a pretty little market town with a magnificent cathedral as the centrepiece to its cobbled square. I set off one overcast morning to the sound of bells ringing. They turned out to be more death knell than fanfare. I followed the footpath that hugged the river, a spring in my step as I imagined all the delights that lay up ahead. I'd never done much serious walking, but I enjoyed a good hike as much as the next man. However, I had travelled to Germany with my Vauxhall Conference League trainers and due to the early morning humidity had decided to go what they call in podiatric circles 'bareback' without socks. It wasn't long before my feet were squelching along as if strapped into Tupperware filled with sugar water. My discomfort reached its zenith somewhere between Ulm and Nordlingen, where I was forced to sit down and inspect how my feet were bearing up. They weren't, even in those few short hours. Both feet were covered in blisters, producing a design that The Future Mapping Company would have been pleased with.

I sat on the bank of the river next to a gnarled old birch tree. At the base of its trunk, carved into the brittle wood, were the letters G. H. I took the letters to be a sign, sent to me from the god of ramblers – 'Go Home!' A short way up ahead from where I'd come to rest was a signpost at a junction: straight on for Regensburg, 66 kilometres, or left turn following a footpath away from the river to Schutzensee, 5 kilometres. I covered up my feet and took the path of least resistance... There had been a change of plan.

I'd never really fully recovered from that particular change of plan. My failure to see more than a glimpse of one of Europe's finest rivers rested uneasily with me, and several years later I was still unsettled by it.

Back to the present and back on the Volga the grey clouds eventually broke, dispensing a light summer rain which kept me company until the early evening. My romantic riverside vision was up for revision. I wanted to keep rowing until the sun began its descent at about seven o'clock. Unfortunately there was no sun to go down, so I simply kept on rowing until suddenly the light went and darkness arrived. The meal I'd fantasised about turned into a packet of cheese biscuits washed down by a cool bottle of Sprite; there wasn't a local to be seen. I slept well for a few hours at least, dozing off beneath a starless sky to the sound of the river's gentle ripples against the bank. I was awoken by the daylight breaking through. There was a sharp chill in the air.

There were few signs of human life on my arrival at Tver some four hours into the day. I dragged *Molly* up a small shingle beach littered with empty beer bottles and plastic bags. I found a convenient wooden post wearily standing upright which I tied *Molly* to with a piece of rope attached to the bow, and made my way to the street. For the first time I felt eyes on me. A handful of sunflower seed squatters glared from the pavement. I cut away from the river at the Stalinist cinema complex and rediscovered my land legs whilst passing through a shabby park complete with a rusty Ferris wheel. People of all ages passed by, some attached to mobile phones, some decorated by chunky headphones. I saw iPods and mountain bikes and a man protectively carrying a dog wrapped in a blanket.

Tver has a rich and – up until recently – progressive history. Situated at the confluence of the Volga and the Tvertsa rivers, the region was once an area of simple woods and bog land, which due to its inaccessibility was spared the Tatar raids and thus received an influx of those escaping from the devastated south. Thanks to its strategic position, it was quickly transformed into one of the wealthiest and most populated of all medieval Russian states. By the end of the thirteenth century Tver was ready to compete with even Moscow for supremacy in Russia.

Unlike his later descendant Ivan the Terrible, Mikhail the Grand Prince of Tver in 1305 was one of the best-loved of all the medieval Russian leaders, not least due to his ongoing resilience against Genghis Khan's all-conquering hordes. He was followed to the throne by son Dmitry, who formed an alliance with the then powerful Grand Duchy of Lithuania, raising Tver's prestige even higher. Prince Ivan of Moscow was furious at the work Dmitry was doing for Tver so engineered his murder – with the help of the Mongols. When the people of Tver heard of the crime they rose up against the Golden Horde, who joined forces with the Muscovites to squash the weak rebellion. This incident proved to be the fatal blow to Tver's aspirations of supremacy in Russia. After a brief resurgence due to another alliance with the Lithuanians, the forces of Ivan the Terrible finally dominated and took the city, at which point it entered a spiral of decline from which it would take centuries to recover.

On the other side of the park was Catherine the Great's pink road house: a majestic remnant of a period when the Czarina chose Tver as her stopover of choice during trips between St Petersburg and Moscow. In the early eighteenth century, Tver gained importance as a principal station on the highway, and later railway, between those two great cities, becoming very popular with Russian royals. A fire in 1763 prompted the thorough rebuilding of the city by Catherine. Crumbling medieval buildings were replaced by imposing neoclassical architecture, most notably Catherine's travel palace designed by the celebrated Matvei Kazakov.

I walked past the statue of Afanasy Nikitin, the explorer, in the shadow of which groups of young men kicked cans, while girls stuttered along the uneven paving in high heels and short summer skirts. Nikitin was a merchant by trade and also one of the first Europeans (after Niccolò de' Conti) to travel to and document his visit to India. During his journey Nikitin studied India's social and military systems, its economy and religion. His material provided a valuable source of information about India at the time. He described his adventure in a book called *The Journey Beyond Three*

Seas. It was a travel diary describing his adventures, which outwardly resembled other tales of pilgrimages to the Holy Land; however, his wasn't a pilgrimage or a journey that involved any amount of piety, so the book stands alone as a work of literature in the fifteenth century. In 1466 Nikitin left Tver on a commercial trip to India. He travelled down the Volga and crossed the Caspian Sea to Persia, where he lived for one year. In 1469 he reached the city of Ormus and then crossed the Arabian Sea to Bahmani Sultanate, which he made his home for the next three years. On his return to Russia he visited Muscat, Somalia and Trabzon. When finally heading back to Tver he died near Smolensk, tragically never making it all the way. It has been said that the true reason for Nikitin's departure for India was to escape the debts he had managed to rack up back in Russia, although he appears not to have done any successful trading once in India. The horse he had taken with him in order to sell was in fact confiscated by a Persian khan who refused to return it until Nikitin had converted to Islam. On his return to Russia he was more in debt than when he had left, but he did have his notes, and in turn his book.

I followed Tverskaya Street to the central train station, opposite which McDonald's appeared through a haze of concrete and scaffold. Inside the fast-food restaurant there was no natural light but it was clean, possessed a fully functioning wash room and the quarter pounders were delicious. Even the staff seemed cheerful in a Ronald McDonald sort of way, i.e. appearing to know something all other inhabitants of the planet didn't. It was like another brightly coloured world, detached from the one beyond the golden arches, a world of homogeny where unashamedly questionable nutrition was purveyed with a smile to those who could afford it, and at this particular red and yellow establishment many could.

The restaurant chain had now had a presence in Russia for some twenty years and had come a long way since the first one provoked mile-long queues in Red Square in the early nineties. Now there were 314 restaurants in 85 different cities across the federation – the great symbol of American culture was now well at home within the borders of the one-time enemy. After a burger and dry chips I enjoyed a glass of Siberian beer whilst considering my first few days on and off the river. I laughed at how I had entertained walking the entire length of the river to the Caspian Sea in two months. My feet were sore after just walking around Tver. I thought about Vicky and all the happiness that awaited me in Astrakhan; it had all become very real now.

Before I'd started the journey Vicky's wedding so far away had been something of an *ignis fatuus*, a chimera that could surely never really evolve into reality. However, now that I was on my way, and the date drew nearer, it was slowly morphing into something that was *very* real. Dmitry and Vicky's relationship (after the initial surprise) had always been a source of joy; they worked effortlessly well together. Rather than create obstacles, the contrast in their backgrounds had strengthened their bond. Despite this, I had never truly believed their relationship would graduate beyond just 'a bit of fun' – two people enjoying a moment in time together, fuelled by the intrigue of the exotic. A beautiful moment caught forever in a bunch of photographs and a few keepsakes, but never anything more. Although I'm not sure there would have been many photographs...

Early on in their courtship Dmitry, never one to shy away from the grand gesture, whisked Vicky off to Paris for a romantic weekend. They sat swigging rosé street side on the Rue Caulaincourt in the shadow of the Sacré-Coeur in Montmartre at the beginning of October. Their legs warmed by blankets and their spirits further warmed by wine as they made plans long into the night, thinking that life couldn't get any better. It did. The following day they grinned their way around the city of light as if high on MDMA, and whilst doing so they soaked up every last drop of the tourist experience. Having purchased sightseeing hop-on hop-off bus tickets, they were hopping about all day. When not marvelling at a city which, courtesy of film and television, they already knew so very well, their daydreams roamed between returning to Paris for the rest of their lives, and the beautiful person they had the unbelievable good fortune to be sitting next to on the top deck as the Eiffel Tower passed by. After what was a perfect three days they were still sipping rosé street side in Montmartre early Sunday evening, weighing up the options of forsaking their Eurostar back to St Pancras and staying put.

Hindsight makes everything easy, and in this case it certainly suggests that by staying put in Paris that night they would have saved themselves considerable bother.

Vicky, unlike Dmitry, was a keen photographer, and as such had recently become the proud owner of a Nikon. Now to those, like me (and Dmitry), who can't tell the difference between an instamatic or an SLR, all you need know is that the Nikon is right up there with the best. This little beauty makes even the most average snapper look like they know what they're doing, and for this very reason, i.e. the ability to turn the mediocre photographer into the gifted, they don't come cheap. Vicky had parted with much hard-earned cash for her splendid new Nikon. Thus it was more than a little disappointing as they sat back on the Eurostar headed for London, whispering sweet nothings and blissfully remembering all the heady detail of their unquestionably wonderful weekend in the world's most romantic city, that it suddenly and with a loud gasp dawned on Vicky that she had left her beloved Nikon on the bed in their pokey little top-floor room at the overpriced and altogether tatty three-star Hotel Roma on the Rue Caulaincourt (it had been neither of the above during their stay).

This was indeed a bad moment. But of course, not just for the loss of the camera. For stealth-like throughout the length of their stay in Paris, largely oblivious to Dmitry – he had been far too full of romance to even notice – Vicky had been snapping away as if all the iconic images that Paris throws up only had a short time left before being taken down and packed away in a box forever. Dmitry suggested he immediately call the hotel, which only made things worse – after going and checking the room, the receptionist could only report that there was no sign of the camera in the room. All those memories, all those perfectly framed pictures now lost, gone, gone, gone... And from that moment on, so was their weekend – there simply was no coming back, no way of rescuing it. And it was small consolation to Vicky, quite understandably, that they still had their own memories – which were far more special than a bunch of snaps everybody has seen everywhere a million times before. Dmitry kept that last bit to himself.

Despite this early disappointment, their relationship survived and had grown stronger. I had been wrong to ever doubt it. Wonderfully dazzling Vicky had fallen in love and I couldn't have been more excited about the prospect of her living happily ever after with Dmitry. This prospect was a great source of inspiration for me to push forward towards Astrakhan, energised by the perfect synchronicity of Vicky and Dmitry's happiness allowing me the opportunity to bathe in the delights of my own adventure. However, I wasn't at McDonald's simply for the burgers and reflection. This was where I had arranged to meet Pasha's brother. I had just finished the last of the beer when a portly man in late middle age passed through the doors, wearing a trilby hat and a check jacket.

After a cursory surveillance of the room, he walked over. Mikhail was a photographer and had been all his life. After the break-up of the Soviet Union he had embarked on a wandering lifestyle that lasted for the next twenty years and led to extended stays in Berlin and southern Ukraine, not to mention a couple of years in London before returning to the place he considered home: Tver. He shook my hand in silence and then settled himself at the table, making sure he was perfectly comfortable before he spoke.

'Pasha said you would like to see some of my photographs.' In contrast to his brother, Mikhail spoke in almost a whisper and appeared timid – his hands gently caressed each other as his piercing blue eyes fixed on my response. In truth I had been curious and had been more interested in meeting Pasha's brother than seeing his photos, but I wasn't going to miss out on the chance to see his work.

'Yes, Pasha said you had an exhibition on at the moment in the town.'

Mikhail chuckled before saying, a little indignantly, 'I always have exhibitions on. During the Soviet times I was an underground artist. Now I am above ground. At the moment I am above ground at the house of culture on Tverskaya, not far from this place... Let's go.' With that, he rose to his feet abruptly and looked about impatiently with an expression on his face that suggested he didn't share my feelings about McDonald's contribution to the world.

Mikhail was a social photographer, a social commentator, before 1991 probably best known for his documentation of poverty and social collapse all over Russia. Since then his work has extended further afield. As we walked at some pace, he gave me some background.

'I became a professional photographer mainly because the Communists didn't like my pictures... or should I say, didn't approve of my photographs.' He now sounded more like his younger brother in tone. 'I lost my job as a factory engineer during the Soviet period when the KGB found nude snaps of my wife... and others.' He glanced my way with the genesis of a smile which came to nothing. 'So the authorities wouldn't let me take any more photos... my photography became something of a protest against the government. I was forced underground, so I had my exhibitions in private apartments, cafes and laundries, we even had one in a kiosk once... There it is, the house of culture.' He gestured towards a faded pink classical building that had appeared in front of us.

Even after the collapse of the Soviet Union, Mikhail continued his protest. With the evolution of the new Russia there was plenty of social commentary to be done and plenty of poverty to document. By the time of its demise, the Soviet Union was left with an army of artists, writers and musicians who simply couldn't react if they wanted to stay alive. Not until its fall could their reaction begin, and Mikhail was a part of that reaction – one that was dramatic, extreme and angry.

Mikhail led me through a small side door into the house of culture. The walls of the nineteenth-century building's grand hallway were decorated by photographs illustrating all three of the above qualities – sepia prints of men and women swimming in lakes brimming over with factory waste; people relaxing and drinking next to rubbish tips. The photographs showed simple pleasures being enjoyed in places contradictory to the idea of pleasure. Mikhail guided me past twenty or so similarly thought-provoking snaps. They were at best gloomy, at worst shocking. At the outset I had considered Mikhail to be the polar opposite of his brother, two very distant personalities brought together by blood. However, now I could see it: they were two halves of the same. Mikhail's art displayed the roots of Pasha's frustrations that were never far from the surface.

Mikhail left me at the originally named Hotel Volga. Without sentiment he touched the rim of his hat and turned away. There was nothing more to say; his pictures had said so much already. The lady on reception, after a surly acknowledgement, took my passport and enough roubles to suggest it was the five-star luxury Hotel Volga. As I went up the spiral stone stairwell it fast became apparent that peak tourist season was the chosen time for renovation. I was soon clambering over stacks of bricks and work benches along a damp-smelling corridor. My room was basic, with a short single bed and a window with a view, although it was debatable how long the view would be available as a wall was being built at the front of the hotel, already high enough to block out the windows on the ground floor. Traffic shook the windows and bed bugs burned my legs, but I slept well that night.

***

The following morning I returned to the shingle beach where I'd left *Molly*. Pasha was already there, perched on the bumper of his 4x4. We heaved the boat from the beach and strapped her onto his roof rack. Once she was secure, as promised Pasha returned the money I'd bought her with, along with the compass he'd tried to sell me those few nights earlier. He had fastened it to some ribbon and placed it around my neck like an Olympic medal, releasing a deep throaty laugh as he did. Still chuckling, he stroked my shoulder and climbed into the Land Cruiser. Starting the engine, he wound down the window and, nodding at the compass, said, 'You need it more than me.' Pasha and *Molly* were soon out of sight and I had a wedding to get to.

CHAPTER TWO

BACK TO THE FUTURE

'How many times in my sorrowful separation,
In my wandering fate,
Have I thought of you, O Moscow!
Moscow... how much there is in this sound
That flows together for the heart of the Russian!'
Alexander Pushkin

Polina had come of age at the beginning of a New Era. She turned eighteen in 1991, the very year in which the Soviet Union heard the fat lady singing. Born into the Brezhnev era, she grew up during the heady days of glasnost and perestroika, until eventually being catapulted into a world of chaos – a future unknown in the Russia of the 1990s. Her parents had never known such uncertainty; paranoia, corrupt leadership and low wages perhaps – but these were things they could be certain of. The world Polina found herself in had no such constants.

Her mother, Galina Salamatova, had been born in 1946 in a small industrial town called Malmyzh, a charmless Soviet administrative centre in the Kirovskiy region of Russia. She had been brought up by her paediatrician mother Margarita, a Labour Veteran of the USSR, ably assisted by her grandmother Yulia, an honoured teacher, and her aunt Vera. Theirs was a proud Soviet home; pictures of both Lenin and Stalin had pride of place on the mantelpiece.

Polina's mother had been an exemplary student and soon became a pioneer member of Komsomol, the youth wing of the Communist Party. The year before she graduated in 1968 she met Alexander Mikhailovich Kuleshov, the cousin of a friend from her institute and they soon fell in love. Alexander was born in 1946 in the village of Beliye Berega, meaning 'white banks', so named because of the white sands that ran along the riverbanks of the village. When they met, Alexander was serving in the Red Army whilst also studying history at the Moscow State Regional University.

In 1969 they married and the young family moved to Moscow, where Galina took a job working in a boarding school for children of artists, musicians and other creative types that wanted to pass on the responsibility of their children's education and everyday life – or simply didn't have the time for it. Meanwhile, Alexander worked as the Komsomol Secretary for a military unit.

In 1970 their first child, Matvey, was born, and in 1973 their second, Polina. With the demise of the Soviet Union and with capitalism flooding in, the Kuleshovs soon took the initiative and founded their own school – such business was booming at that time in Russia. Their business didn't boom for long and after a few difficult years they abandoned the big city and moved to Yaroslavl. Polina went on to study in a classical high school, which offered, quite unusually in Russia, classes in choreography, knitting and cooking, amongst other traditional pursuits. It was a kind of experimental school based on the educational traditions of the nineteenth century; Polina now bakes a very good carrot cake. She entered the history department of the Lomonosov Moscow State University, where she graduated, soon afterwards making her way to the United Kingdom. I had first met Polina when she and her husband had shared the same corner shop as me in Brighton, and on hearing their Russian chat I'd seen a golden opportunity to practise mine whilst buying a pint of semi-skimmed. It wasn't long before they were showing me photos of the motherland over Russian liquorice and Lipton's Yellow Label tea. Unfortunately their marriage didn't last much longer than the liquorice and Polina eventually found her way back to Russia.

***

Sparks flew as the long metallic arm obediently followed the cable. Trolleybus 301 juddered down an uneven potholed street, past the faded ochre paintwork of a pre-Soviet technical college propped up on either side by grey apartment blocks like giant concrete bookends. Past a post office the road opened up into a grandiose square where the red, white and blue of the national flag danced high on skinny poles around the centrepiece fountains. The bus then swung into a steep, winding, cobbled road which penetrated the heart of the town. Shabby houses coloured blue, green and grey, shaded by trees indiscriminately rising up from the cracked and worn pavement, gave way to more solid concrete buildings. These were fronted by shops, bakeries, mobile phone sellers and banks, and punctuated by gaps that gave views of high-rise Soviet estates. The faded colours gave rise to sharp and brightly primary ones, softened by dust from the street and the smoke bellowing from car exhausts, as I made my way to meet Polina.

On leaving Pasha and *Molly* in Tver, I had taken a local train to Moscow's Yaroslavsky Station, in order to catch another train to another Moscow satellite town, Yaroslavl, where I would rejoin the Volga. The train had stopped many times on its route to the capital, even at platforms with no visible sign of existence in any direction, for invisible passengers to embark and disembark. Snapshots of a rural Russia flew past my dusty window in stark contradiction to the orgy of human life that awaited in Moscow. Lush pastures were punctuated by scrappy woodlands of silver birch and beech. Old barns sat forgotten and lonely on hillsides. Ticket collectors had come and gone; with their approach whole carriages had been deserted, as fare dodgers had abandoned the train to run the entire length of platforms, rejoining the train further along.

Once in Moscow, I had crossed the Komsomolskaya Square into the Kazansky Station, one of the capital's nine stations, built between 1913 and 1940. The white stone carvings that decorate its brick walls give it a magnificence in line with eighteenth-century Russian architectural traditions. I dodged an army of taxi drivers touting for business at the entrance before spending several hours snoozing in a chair within the imperial majesty of the waiting lounge. My neighbour was a man of few words, but occasionally he altered position, scratched a part of his body and smiled at me inanely. When the putrid smell of his bare feet had become overwhelming I looked to caffeine to help kill some time, before going walkabout.

Love Moscow or hate it, and many do both at the same time, it is impossible not to feel excited by it. Perhaps this is simply because the city's physical appearance is constantly in a state of transition. Demolition lives alongside furious construction as Moscow experiments with different styles – whole streets might change with the blink of an eye. Forgotten wastelands are watched over by recently built skyscrapers, which the very next week might have swapped places. The city can boast Europe's tallest block of flats, the most billionaires and the most expensive cup of coffee, but that might not be the case tomorrow. It's often been called a collection of villages, and as you walk around this is evident behind the veneer of cosmopolitan sophistication. It began life as a provincial outpost in 1147, expanding in all directions from the Kremlin that was then and still remains Moscow's heart. As this expansion took place, the new districts took on their own, often very particular identities based on the inhabitants. Kitai Gorod, or Chinatown, was to become a centre of trade, home to merchants and craftsmen. Zamoskvorechie was the district where those who serviced the royal court set up home. The streets around Tverskoy attracted the eighteenth-century nobility, whereas the Arbat drew the artists and writers who were to become the nineteenth-century intellectual elite. Moscow is a window onto Russia's contrasts; it is where extreme poverty sits next to oligarchic wealth, crumbling churches beside shimmering corporate skyscrapers. It's not always easy on the eye – aesthetically, it compares unfavourably to Petersburg in the north – but it's a living city and, as such, its spirit comes more than anywhere from the Muscovites.

The highlight of my four-hour ride north from Moscow to Yaroslavl was the stop I made at Sergiev Posad, although the lady sitting in the seat opposite who passed the journey whittling a uniquely proportioned potato came a close second. The Trinity Monastery of St Sergius is considered to be one of the most important spiritual sites in all Russia. It was founded in 1340 by the country's one-time most revered saint, St Sergius of Rodonezh. Hundreds of pilgrims and tourists visit the town every day now. So about a third of the way to Yaroslavl I left my whittling companion and joined the tourist trail, not to miss out on the chance of some spiritual enlightenment.

Tourists behave in strange ways. The minute they set foot in pastures new an unwritten contract is signed that states all the checks and balances that define their 'normal' existence are no longer legitimate. The grey-haired man only metres away was no exception, as I watched him exchange the equivalent of five pounds sterling for a small bottle of water. With said bottle firmly in his grasp and the transaction complete, he had profusely thanked the daylight robber who had taken his money, with a smile on his face that suggested no hint of scepticism, rather that he had just been in receipt of the keys to paradise. A few years before, I'd met a young commercial lawyer from Chertsey, whilst passing through the Siberian city of Tomsk. We had been staying at the same hotel and had passed some time together over tea in the hotel's lobby, during which time he had confirmed his status as a tourist whilst returning from a conference in China. We parted company after our brief and polite interlude which had left me considering that a more conscientious lawyer and altogether polished ambassador for the United Kingdom I was unlikely to meet. Later that night on my way to bed after a sedate evening spent dining in the hotel lounge followed by a stroll around the local environs, I passed him running through the hotel reception dressed only in Y-fronts, whilst singing 'Bring Me Sunshine' out of key. The 'othered' world of the tourist was indeed a strange place, and one that people found themselves in completely of their own volition. Nobody is forced to go on holiday. Nobody is forced to leave the safe and familiar environment that is home to become a tourist.

Outside the main ticket office for the Trinity Monastery of St Sergius, the camera-wielding sightseers were no different, eager to divine their very own enlightenment from this foremost site of spirituality. Groups of predominantly East Asians jockeyed for positions that day. Some calmly stood whilst being addressed by guides or group leaders, safe in the knowledge that all responsibility had been relinquished, and thus the job of getting them in to see the country's foremost spiritual site and tourist attraction was somebody else's. Others appeared more agitated as they tried to hold position in a queue that had no obvious design and was prone to regular sabotage from new arrivals. Those who had already passed through the heavy wrought-iron gates gathered, with expressions of relief fused with expectation, for what was now within grasp. Coach after coach appeared and swung alongside the fence that ran the length of the complex, allowing more and more tourists to disembark in preparation for one of the highlights of their Imperial Russian sightseeing orgy.

A few locals passed by, distinguished by their nonchalance, the occasional glance, perhaps a look of disdain. Others were able to see the visitors for what (on the whole) they indeed were, a bona fide source of revenue. They knew that in amongst the collective of tourists stomping through their town there would be at least one who would without question buy a matryoshka doll or a T-shirt decorated with Putin superimposed onto an ostrich for something close to a 100 per cent markup. They knew that there would be at least one who would pay three times as much for a bottle of water because it suddenly appeared in front of them, rather than the amount they would have to pay if they had taken the time to visit a shop. They knew that souvenirs made tourists behave in strange ways, often quite unpredictably. These weren't just T-shirts or wooden dolls. The tourists with lots of money and patronising manners were buying memories, investing in their futures and the futures of generations to come, and the Russians that looked on with smiles on their faces knew that you couldn't put a price on that.

Souvenir Alley, located across the road from the main ticket office, was a narrow lane running some half a mile on a gentle incline swamped with stalls purveying souvenirs of all imagined shapes and sizes. The Russians waited with anticipation for the arrival of the next tour group that would run the gauntlet through the collection of overpriced homogenised memories for sale. At the bottom end, coaches gathered to take them on to the next sight. The vendors chatted, smoked and busily reorganised their displays. All the stalls were colourful, offering the necessary amount of gentle seduction. The truth was that it was more a case of chance whether or not a tourist chose to part with their money at any particular stall. It was more about the variables influencing that split-second decision to buy.

I found a little pop-up cafe at the top end of the alley and, with a coffee, I waited too as a group fresh from the delights of the monastery started to filter into the alley. I watched as they sized up the scene ahead of them, whilst the vendors nonchalantly sized up the approaching horde, clicking away as they ambled or stumbled ahead. There was no hard sell going on here; the souvenir sellers were hardened and not least aware that there was very little science as to why a purchase might be made from them rather than their neighbour with exactly the same display.

At first tentative, the tourists then grew in confidence. This wasn't like a north African bazaar, but probably the antithesis. The occasional gently spoken 'You're welcome' could be heard, accompanied by a softly guiding hand, but on the whole there wasn't any verbal interaction. The bottleneck gradually evened out as some tourists, seeing the coaches assembled, speeded on, while others loitered and others touched, stroked and appeared interested in the goods on offer. One or two looked like they had unwittingly crossed over into enemy lines and, somewhat disorientated, could only think of escape. Others still hungry for visual memories snapped away at anything that moved or breathed with their cameras. A couple of young men even took a picture of me drinking coffee. Not to miss out, I took a picture of them taking a picture of me drinking coffee and in so doing created the tourism equivalent of a hall of mirrors. A line of photographers, furiously still snapping the monastery, stood firm as if they were the last stand of a colonial army holding back an onslaught from native warriors. After fifteen minutes of furious activity it was possible to see the last of this group climb the steps up into their coach. The calm after the storm descended, but not for long – the next group soon approached, and then another, and then another.

THE TRINITY CATHEDRAL

The heart of the monastery is the Trinity Cathedral, modelled on the cathedral of the same name in the Moscow Kremlin. It was finished in 1585 with money that had been left by Ivan the Terrible – a bequest owing to a fit of remorse suffered by Ivan having just killed his own son. St Sergius himself was soon named Russia's patron saint after his death at the age of 78, which would be considered a ripe old age in today's Russia, but in the fourteenth century there must have been something in the water.

On my way back to the station I was joined by a short man with a stick, who began a prolonged bout of arm tapping and grunting and general invasion of my personal space, like some overgrown child with a sugar craving. After a couple of minutes, hovering between aggression and pathos, the skinny man was undeterred, his repetitious imprecations now transposed into a fractious wail of protest, his arms now grabbing hold of my arms and tugging. The tugging then became a clawing action, its rhythms synchronised with the undulations of the wailing, both building to an intensity that suggested the man's life hung in the balance for want of a few roubles – money that I didn't actually have in my pocket. I began to think weakly that perhaps his life really was in peril. I attempted to calm the man and to disengage his clutching hands from my arm. It was no easy task; my assailant had whipped himself into a kind of frenzied trance, like a whirling dervish, for which presumably only the administration of some small change was the antidote. The frenzy was now evolving into something resembling an epileptic fit. Tears were now falling from his eyes and the wailing was sounding more like something from a natural history programme. This all went on for what seemed like an age – until a smartly dressed man with a briefcase brushed past us both. This had the immediate effect of silencing my tormentor's wailing and he soon released his desperate grip from my arm. Released, I instinctively broke into a jog until clear of the monastery's environs. Glancing back over my shoulder, I saw the beggar dangling what appeared to be his full weight from the arm of the man who had unwittingly saved me, with Russia's most spiritual site as a backdrop.

Having rejoined a train for Yaroslavl, staring out the window at lush grassland, I felt a little tinge of disappointment that I hadn't been able to muster the energy to get myself through the gates and inside the monastery. I just hadn't had the stomach for the fight that was necessary to buy a ticket. Perhaps some things are just easier with a group leader. I also realised how thirsty I was and that at that moment in time I would have paid a king's ransom for a bottle of water.

***

Lavish new flowerbeds, freshly painted façades and the occasional stretch of newly paved sidewalk were just a few of the ways the local government was spending money in Yaroslavl. Staying true to the strong Soviet belief of impression management, the cosmetic exterior of the town centre was in good shape. The bus pulled alongside the green and white building of the Cbet Bank, where I caught sight of the small sign for the 'Cafe Red'. I walked through an underpass beneath the road – complete with a singing lady in the musty semi-darkness. I was soon overwhelmed by the aroma of ground coffee being peddled by a man in plus fours.

I emerged quite nauseous at the entrance to a narrow passageway leading into a courtyard, complete with a cafe terrace and quirky boutiques selling abstract artwork. Beyond large wooden saloon doors the scene was much like an English tea room, contrary to the Communist sympathy the name of the cafe suggested. The large cork noticeboard by the door was littered with linguistic suggestion, invitations to 'Learn Russian', language exchanges, language classes, language meet ups, accommodation for speakers of foreign languages –

in fact just about anything you could do with language was on offer, as well as some offers that didn't involve opening your mouth, such as 'city walks'. On the wall next to the board hung a copy of a portrait of Sergey Diaghilev, the Marinsky Ballet's impresario. The original, painted by Leon Brakst, is now on display in the Russian Museum.

A soft voice disturbed me from my surveillance of the surroundings. The utterance came from a small table, nestled in between two tall, bulging bookshelves. Polina sat alone but for a frothy coffee and an upturned paperback in front of her. Slight, with long brown hair and conspicuously pale features, she smiled warmly as I joined her at the table.

'So you made it!' she exclaimed, as if my arrival had been in doubt. Polina carried an authority that made her seem older than her years. A frothy latte she had been quick to order for me soon arrived at the table, courtesy of a man dressed in board shorts.

Polina had offered her services as a 'fixer'. She had proposed to help me sort out onward transport from Yaroslavl should I need it, which I had assumed to mean the purchase of bus tickets, train tickets, that sort of thing. I did need her assistance, but my plan didn't involve parting with any money. I was going to try to complete the next leg without buying anything, travelling to Nizhni Novogorod with the minimum of expense, inspired by the Russian Free Travel Foundation (RFTF), an organisation that encourages and promotes travelling on the cheap or for free around the federation. To this end I was hoping Polina would be able to make good an introduction for me to somebody driving to Novogorod. She was clearly keen to show me the fruit of her labours so, having impatiently waited for me to finish my coffee, she rose from her chair saying, 'We have to meet with Olev.'

TWO YAROSLAVL SUPERLATIVES

By population, Yaroslavl is the largest town on the Volga's journey since its genesis back at Volgaverkhovye. The city is situated in the central area of the East European Plain, also known as the Russian Plain, which is the largest mountain-free part of all the European landscape. The plain spans 4 million square kilometres and averages about 170 metres in elevation. The highest point of the plain is in the Valdai Hills close to the source of the Volga. Its boundaries include the White Sea and the Barents Sea in the north, the Ural Mountains, the Ural River and the Caspian Sea to the east, the Caucasus Mountains and the Black Sea to the south and to the west the Baltic Sea. Yaroslavl is the oldest of all the current towns on the river, with little in the way of competition, having been founded by Yaroslavl the Wise at some point between 988 and 1010.

Meeting Olev required a short bus ride towards the outskirts of town. On leaving the bus we passed through an underpass decorated with anti-war slogans such as 'No War Peace' scribbled onto the concrete walls in yellow paint alongside CND symbols. The indomitable words 'Give peace a chance' were also present. I wasn't convinced that these sentiments aligned comfortably with current Russian leadership's attitudes, but they added much-needed colour to an otherwise gloomy subway. By way of contrast, the word 'Doom' was painted in blood red next to a swastika.

Emerging from the tunnel we were greeted by daylight and a small park. A young woman was perched on some steps silhouetted by the sun. As we got closer it became apparent she was manning a stall, purveying an eclectic selection for children: plastic windmills, plastic raincoats, cuddly bags and cuddly toys. Written on the wall close by, with an arrow pointing in her direction, was the Russian word *Magazene*, meaning 'shop', successfully drawing attention to her entrepreneurial efforts. Directly above the word for shop, and for reasons less logical, was the universally recognised collocation 'Modder Fokker'. Oblivious to the suspect signage, a mother dragged her young daughter over and started rummaging through the merchandise.

On the other side of the park there was a small cluster of wooden izbas, which we soon arrived in amongst. In an area cut off by a steaming sewage pipe, which a family of kittens warmed themselves beneath, we found Olev's residence. Polina led us to what looked like a garden shed painted bright blue and green. In the dusty yard out front, on an upturned crate, sat a thick-set man smoking a cigarette. 'Olev?' Polina asked timidly. She had been given the tip about Olev from one of her students. A rather vapid greeting ensued before he led us into his shed. Once under cover, Olev became more animated. He pushed his chest out and with an air of pride gazed with admiration at the object we had formed a semicircle around.

What we were looking at was an old bicycle. It had two wheels, check, a frame, check, and even a basket on the front. A rusty bell, soon demonstrated by Olev, more than compensated for the lack of brakes (whilst stationary, anyway).

'I built her myself,' Olev exclaimed with glee.

I figured he was simply easing me into his company by showing off his hobby, before we had the opportunity for closer bonding within the confines of his car. Or was something else afoot? My concerns began to bubble when it was suggested I give Olev's bicycle a test ride. When money was mentioned my red alert went off, more specifically regarding the sum of fifty dollars that Olev wanted for the old bike. At that point it became crystal clear that wires at some stage had been significantly crossed. I had wanted to do the next leg of the journey on the cheap, avoiding train tickets and bus tickets, but also avoiding my own man power. I wanted a lift, not a bicycle. Nizhni Novogorod was 360 kilometres away and I was fairly confident that was 360 kilometres too far for me to travel on a bike. Olev repeated 'Fifty dollars' followed by his belief that it was a very good price. Several moments passed with Olev watching the confusion seep across my entire face and then when he decided I'd suffered enough he joyfully expounded, 'I'm joking of course. I make these things from junk I find and then sell them.' Well I had fallen for that, a knowing look from Polina adding confirmation if it had been necessary.

Bicycles weren't the only thing Olev made from bits and bobs he found discarded; he was quite the recycler. He went on to show us a leather cap he'd made from an old punch bag he'd found in the park, and a bottle opener of sorts. He was also quite the businessman and was happy to give me a lift 'some of the way' if I could contribute approximately the value of the bicycle. I wasn't really in a position to argue, and as Polina had gone to the trouble of finding him, I reluctantly agreed. I could have taken a bus for the same amount. An inauspicious beginning for my free-travel aspirations!

* * *

Polina hailed the first yellow cab to pass by. We were going out to celebrate because:

1. It was Polina's birthday.
2. I was in town.
3. Does there have to be a reason?

We were not long in the taxi when the driver produced, with a hoarse chuckle, a dubious-looking potion from beneath a greasy rag in his utility box, and we both cautiously took a sip. I choked; Polina smiled before sipping some more. We left the centre of town and climbed a narrow street lined with old imperial-style mansions. Within five minutes the taxi pulled over and deposited us on a deserted street. We stood at the top of a set of uneven stone steps which led down to a basement, listening to the stifled beats of techno music. We descended the steps and Polina burst through the door in a way that you do when you know exactly what to expect on the other side. We were entering an old apartment that had been in Polina's family for decades. It had been unoccupied for some years now – but lent itself as the perfect venue for social events and anything else for which it might be required. The audio cocktail of singing and laughter engulfed us. Opposite the door a fire roared with a cluster of people gathered around it. A stout wooden table in the middle of the space supported a lone dancer flailing his limbs in all directions whilst spraying beer from a large jug over himself and anybody else close by. Baskets filled with brightly coloured flowers dangled from chains attached to either end of an old yoke mounted above the sole window, through which the street was now partially visible in the half-light of the post-sunset city.

Adjacent to the doorway was a substantial slab of pine resting on four empty beer crates: the bar. A plump man wearing an ill-fitting waistcoat, shirt sleeves rolled up, was on tending duty. He busily opened beer bottles and poured shots. A woman wearing a flowing patterned dress and a scarf that held back her greying hair collected the ready shots on a silver platter and distributed them amongst the other revellers.

THE LIFE AND TIMES OF RUSSIAN VODKA

It was noted by a certain nineteenth-century writer that vodka made its first appearance in Russia in 1398 when the Genoese began shipping it to Lithuania. However, it wasn't until the mid-1400s that distillation actually began in Russia. Not long after, the state had a monopoly on vodka production – a stranglehold that was to last for some four hundred years. During this time, vodka became a vital part of Russian culture, as it both financed the Russian state and destroyed people's lives through alcoholism and drinking-related accidents. There wasn't any time or place in Russian society that vodka was not accepted and welcomed, whether at home or the workplace, for breakfast, lunch or dinner.

Over one hundred different vodkas are now available in Russia. Beer has always been a popular drink, yet invariably it comes an inadequate second to vodka due to its inability to pack the punch necessary to unleash the desired Slavic passions. Beer is more suited to the Brits and Germans, who are less prone to releasing passion of any kind. In 986 Grand Prince Vladimir rejected Islam as the state religion on the grounds that it prohibited alcohol consumption. He once said, 'For the Rus, drink is joy – we cannot be without it.'

The earliest vodka was flavoured to hide the many impurities that found their way into the drink through the crude early distilling processes. As the processes became more sophisticated, rye instead of wheat or potatoes became the grain of choice, which greatly reduced the number of medieval Russians losing their eyesight. By the 1700s, triple distilling with birch charcoal filtering became the standard for finer vodkas – which made flavouring unnecessary. In the twenty-first century the finest Russian vodka is defined as 'that using Moscow waters, distilled from grain and diluted to a concentration of 40% ABV', and lovingly referred to by many Russians as 'the devil's piss'.

I was introduced to Polina's parents, who came out from behind the makeshift bar, and I offered a hand to shake. The gesture was met by laughter bellowing from Alexander's mouth; he then pushed my hand aside and enveloped me in a mighty bear hug, dispatching my temperate gesture with the indignation it deserved and squeezing me close to hyperventilation. I'm pretty sure at one point I saw stars. Fortunately he was distracted from his assault by the arrival of a fresh box of vodka bottles onto the bar, which he began to plunder with the gusto of a man with moments to live. Galina's greeting was gentler, kissing me lightly on both cheeks whilst patting my head.

It wasn't long before I'd been dragged up onto the table with the lone dancer, who insisted on pouring beer over both our heads. I took that to be a signal to throw my own appendages about with reckless abandon. Seeing me tangle myself into a beer-soaked knot, Polina eventually came and rescued me and took me over to the fireplace, where introductions began in earnest. Her uncle, sharing her father's plump rosy cheeks but attached to a body half the size, wore his boots Cossack-style and at intervals would threaten a jig of sorts by raising a knee and grabbing the arm of the nearest person to him. Polina's brother, a lanky guy with a bushy mop of dark hair, was keen for me to balance a jug of beer on both knees and my head at the same time, having proffered a full demonstration. I wasn't able to get further than the second knee, much to his irritation, and probably spilt about a barrel of beer trying. Eventually he gave up and told me he'd just settle for a rendition of my favourite Russian song, but soon lost interest in me completely, much preferring to show off his beer-jug-on-knee balancing skills. There were grandparents, aunts and cousins present, and the guy who lived in the flat above. Other party goers included Helena, who only seemed to say one thing and with her hand over her mouth: 'I can't talk as I'm far too drunk.' Then there was Sveta, who, whenever the uncle cracked a joke, whether it was rib-splittingly funny or not (and most things were by then), punched him with all her strength in the gut. It never became clear why she did this – in fact it must have hurt, but the older man managed to laugh and choke it off every time.

As the party moved around the room, one person remained unmoved by the fireside, a dark-skinned man called Talik. He was taking some time off from his all-night shop, not far away. He sat on a stool so close to the hearth that every now and again a flame leapt out and appeared to lick his face. I took the opportunity to talk to him as the rest of the gathering danced to a familiar folk song. I pulled up a seat and he had soon filled my empty glass. He circled the rim of his glass with his thumb whilst looking at me with his clear blue eyes, chinked my glass and then under his breath said, 'To friendship.' The warm alcohol hit my throat and in turn sank me deeper into my stool, leaving me lost in the flames and their games. I found myself again when he asked, 'So what are you doing here?' I told him about the trip along the river. 'Aah, yes, a pilgrimage along our mother Volga,' he said, and paused before adding, 'This is like a Russian climbing to the top of Big Ben.' I thought about this comparison and wasn't altogether sure that I agreed with him.

THE LIFE AND TIMES OF RUSSIAN VODKA CONTINUED

It was Ivan the Terrible who was responsible for building the first *kabak* or tavern in Moscow. During his 1552 siege of Kazan he had seen Tartar *kabaki*, and stole the idea of state-owned distilleries and *kabaki* as a way to control the vodka trade whilst at the same time profiting from it. Of course, with the rise in the number of *kabaki* came a rise in drunkenness. The state's stranglehold on vodka production continued until 1861, which saw reforms providing something of a hiatus from the monopoly – it didn't last long, but just long enough for some bloke called Pierre Smirnoff to make his fortune in the distilling trade.

In the twentieth century, 40 per cent of all state revenue came from alcohol duty and sales. The Russian population has always been very obliging in its large vodka consumption and not surprisingly the state has only ever encouraged their enthusiasm. Between 1940 and 1985 vodka production doubled, and in roughly the same period alcohol consumption in the Soviet Union quadrupled. One study estimated that 15 per cent of the population in the eighties could be called alcoholic. Alcohol became the biggest cause of divorce and 74 per cent of all murders committed were under the influence. The state's dependence on revenues still encourages the people's dependence on alcohol. By 1995 the combined death toll from alcohol poisoning, cirrhosis and alcohol-induced violence equalled some 500 deaths per 100,000; 43,000 Russians die each year from vodka poisoning alone. More recently, measures have been taken to try to combat the problem – measures that have included the minimum price of a bottle of vodka being doubled. However, even more recently, the financial crisis in Russia has led to proposals that the minimum price of vodka be lowered.

These statistics were a million miles from my thoughts as all around me in this modern-day kabak, vodka was being consumed like it was going out of production. Outwardly nobody was dying, only having more life-affirming fun than I could imagine possible.

A large glug of cognac, and Talik continued. Although I can't be sure what he said due to the noise and the cognac, it was roughly along these lines: 'The river has seen it all: growth, life and prosperity, war, death and industry. It is a life source unto itself, a living breathing entity. She is truly one of the founding arteries of Russia.'

After a few moments I noticed that Talik had moved close, his hand resting on my knee, his mouth eventually uttering the words 'Good night'. He rose from his seat, knocked back what was left in his glass and threw the empty into the flames. He then crossed the room and without so much as an adieu left through the heavy door into the night. The dancing had come to an end. It was time for us to go as well. After a repeat of the hugs and kisses that had greeted us, and sincere invitations to return, we climbed the steps from the basement into a night fast conceding to the day. I walked arm in arm with Polina back to the centre, the numbed clarity of a night's drinking pushing us wearily along past fellow merrymakers, drunks and lovers and more drunks and lovers.

* * *

The following morning I joined Polina in the kitchen of her second-floor flat for breakfast. Over sweet tea and

Belarusian rye bread with cheese, my host shared with me her views on marriage along with some insights into the route I'd be travelling. Beyond Nizhni Novogorod I would be passing through Kazan. Polina had been there once as a child but had no recollection of it; further south she had never been. She was able to tell me that Samara, which was on my planned route, came alive in summer, so I would be visiting at the best time. Regarding the subject of marriage, despite the generosity of her enthusiasm for the wedding I was heading towards, with regards to herself she was unable to do much more than shake her head and tut quite a lot.

Olev had arranged to pick me up at around nine o'clock that morning. I had been slightly dubious, so I was pleasantly surprised when Polina received a call at nine on the dot; however, I was not surprised to hear Olev's voice booming down the phone, 'I have problem with the car – we will leave at eleven.' Several cups of tea later and nearer twelve than eleven, a horn from the street below sounded.

Only a short way into my Volga journey and I had already said 'goodbye' a few times. Parting with anyone I never found particularly comfortable, unable to gauge the required level of investment needed for the gesture in any given situation. I tended to overthink 'goodbyes'. Even the most straightforward parting of ways I found myself clumsily mismanaging. On this occasion, as Polina casually presented a cheek ready for a kiss, I found my hand hovering awkwardly waiting for a shake... We settled for a bungled fusion of both kiss and shake.

Farewells out of the way, I clambered into the Volga Sedan saloon. Olev crunched it into gear, released the handbrake and rolled the antiquated engine into life. We chugged through the city streets, through the suburbs and beyond the edge of town along a cratered road, by the side of which crows and rooks wrestled with plastic bags. As we broke from the city Olev gave out a prolonged bronchial cough as if to confirm that the air was now cleaner. Then with an open road ahead he put his foot down... but not for long. Progress at speed lasted for approximately five minutes and about three kilometres. He then slowed right down and came to a halt by the side of the road.

'Okay, this is where I stop,' he said nonchalantly. A look of what must have been utter disbelief came over my face as his words from the day before slammed like a runaway juggernaut into my head: 'I will take you some of the way for fifty dollars.' Seeing that I was more than a little surprised, he added, 'Don't worry, a truck will be along soon; this is a good place.'

I looked around. His words did offer some consolation as the road was busy, and wet as it had started raining. There was no point in arguing, as Olev's tone had left no doubt that this was where he was indeed stopping, so I dragged myself from the car and shut the door, unable even to thank him, still in a state of mild stupefaction. At that moment all I could think was how badly I had let the free travel movement down.

I started tentatively walking, thumb aloft at the end of an outstretched arm, battling with heavy freight trucks roaring past, blowing me from side to side and covering me in spray. A few hours in and I'd actually forgotten about the river, finding a lift and the wedding – my entire focus was on staying alive. Still, when a lorry with Murmansk plates slid to a halt some twenty metres up the road, my initial thoughts were of relief – relief that I could now proceed in warmth and safety.

I wasn't to experience either of the above sensations anytime soon. The driver leapt from his cab waving his hands around and yelling expletives, making it quickly clear that he wasn't St Christopher in the guise of a Russian trucker. In an attempt to defuse the oncoming tirade I persuaded myself that he was merely very kindly advising that the road was too dangerous for hitch-hiking and that I'd be much better off joining him in his truck. By the time he had reached me, my thoughts had re-entered the world of reality with stark clarity – he was very angry and no amount of wishful thinking was going to persuade me otherwise.

When confronted by angry men, or women for that matter (although pretty much without exception it is the men driving trucks in Russia), I play the idiot. This is a role I have mastered over the years. My antagonist can wave their arms and yell until they convulse with exhaustion; however, I generally find the moment they realise that there is a very good chance I *am* an idiot, i.e. a foreigner who doesn't understand them or the ways of their country, they will concede to saving energy and retreat with a few unconsidered expletives. Now, Russian expletives could easily fill their own Concise Dictionary of Russian Expletives (there might even be one) but on this occasion my protagonist had clearly only read a small section of said dictionary and was hell-bent on repeating it – perhaps just to confirm he'd read it. The watered-down version goes something like this:

'You stupid idiot! You stupid idiot! You stupid idiot!'

The gist was that he believed unequivocally that it wasn't a suitable stretch of road for hitch-hikers and that I shouldn't really be there. Needless to say, the ensuing scene was not attractive. The trucker had gone to the trouble of stopping so he was going to get his money's worth. It wouldn't have mattered if I were an idiot, or Putin, or a goat standing forlornly by the side of the road. I took a proper verbal hammering. It would have been pointless to share with my abuser that I had indeed had my own misgivings about travelling along the road anyway – this man wasn't listening. Just as it crossed my mind that he probably wouldn't be satisfied until I was injured in some way, and therefore unable to continue, he backed off – spitting at his feet as he marched back to his abandoned vehicle. It was with more than a little relief that I saw his truck vanish over the horizon.

I considered what had just occurred. Then I sat down and considered myself and what I was doing and why I was doing it. I was making life much harder for myself than it needed to be, there was a perfectly good bus service (well... alright, not 'perfectly' good, but the train service was), yet a series of questionable decisions had led me to the side of a pot-holed and soon-to-be-waterlogged road in western Russia. Then, probably more consideration than necessary at that point took me into a deep appraisal of the benefits of not doing what I was doing. Then I noticed I was shaking.

I found myself withdrawing from the road, dragging my legs over rough scrub and ravines full of muddy brown rainwater, before settling myself on the edge of a ditch. I sunk effortlessly into the soft clay, sucked in. Probably the sensible thing to do was to return to Yaroslavl and proceed on the next warm and dry train east to Nizhni Novogorod, and this did cross my mind... but that's all it did.

I was on a particular stretch of the Volga that has over the years inspired so much music, literature and art that it is often considered the cradle of Russian art – although at that point I was oblivious to any such inspiration. The Tartar satirist Mikhail Saltykov Shchedrin was born in Tver, though he spent much of his life not far from Kostroma, only a stone's throw away. However, it was Alexander Ostrovsky who had had possibly the most intimate relationship with the Volga. Widely considered to be the greatest representative of the Russian realistic period, he wrote 47 original plays. *The Storm*, which was turned into an opera, *Katya Kabanova*, is the story of two young lovers, their relationship, and in turn their relationship with the Volga. The headstrong and passionate heroine meets her end by throwing herself into the river, the river being the only real home for such a restless spirit.

In 1856 Ostrovsky made his own journey along this part of the river from Tver to Nizhni Novogorod as part of a government-sponsored economic survey at the start of the reign of Czar Alexander II, prior to the Czar's landmark emancipation of the serfs in 1861. He went on to publish some travel notes that he had made about his journey; these were essentially background to *The Storm*. I wondered if Ostrovsky had made the trip by foot or simply had had better luck finding a lift.

Dragging myself into an upright position and beginning to walk, I screamed for some small piece of good fortune.

The god of luck had woken up when I arrived back at the road. Not one but two trucks were stationary in the lay-by where I'd had my earlier altercation. I wasted no time in approaching the first, a huge articulated beast of the road with what a cursory appraisal suggested had plenty of room in the cab. The driver was fast asleep; I could hear his snoring from the roadside. I banged furiously on the door, but he slept on quite oblivious. A little agitated now as I saw the early threads of my plan disintegrating, I moved on to the second of the lorries. Music blared from the cab, some variant on traditional Irish music – could I have hit on an Irishman? I yelled a greeting over the sound of the fiddles and was greeted with a sleepy smile from the occupant – who introduced himself as Sergey and wasn't Irish.

After I explained my predicament and shamefully, going against the philosophy of the free travel movement, even offered a small fee, Sergey ushered me into the passenger seat, confirming that we would be in Nizhni Novogorod before nightfall. Once I was safely ensconced, he told me that he had spent the last ten years of his life careering around Russia's suspect road infrastructure, so much so that probably his true home was now on the road. I asked him what his family thought about that.

'I have no family now,' was his curt response. 'I am divorced and my son has his own family.'

I asked him where he went when he wasn't driving.

'I am always driving.' As I looked around his cab, his words were confirmed. If you took away the steering wheel and gearstick, it could have quite easily been a bedsit, and he had made it very homely with a TV set, photos and other paraphernalia. He even had a crudely put-together drinks cabinet next to the mini fridge, from which he soon dug out a couple of bottles of beer.

When he found out where I was from, he began shaking his head and telling me: 'Ooh, Russia very dangerous.' Russians the world over love people to think their country is the most dangerous, though I knew that it was probably no more dangerous than anywhere else. It is probably true to say their roads are, however. Russia has about 933,000 kilometres of 'road', but road safety in Russia is poor, to put it mildly, with road accident deaths higher than in any other country of the G8, although less than in China and India. How anybody knows this I don't know, but apparently the level of risk in using a Russian road is 60 times greater than that of Great Britain.

That said, the road density is the lowest of all the G8 countries; you can travel for days without passing another road user. The road to Nizhni could therefore be considered relatively busy, as we consistently passed other vehicles, mainly articulated trucks ploughing their course. Before leaving for Russia I had stupidly watched a YouTube clip of a Russian truck careering head on into a huge tractor trailer. The driver hurtles head-first through the windscreen of his cab, miraculously lands on his feet, scratches his head and walks away apparently unscathed. I think this kind of luck only strikes once. It was briefly questioned in the comments section why he wasn't wearing a seat belt, before comments on the quality of his dismount dominated.

The miles flew by to a soundtrack of Russian pop, punctuated by expletives and Sergey's family history, punctuated by more expletives – usually directed at the condition of the road, or the performance of other road users. My benefactor, a stranger only hours before, I got to know pretty well very quickly. Sergey was good company and certainly seemed glad of some company himself.

'My dad was a crane operator who liked fishing on the Volga and drinking vodka – usually at the same time,' he chuckled unconvincingly. 'My mother was a cleaner – neither could understand why I was interested in mathematics.' I was a little surprised myself by this declaration. 'But they were pleased for me when I won a place at the Moscow Institute of Physics and Technology.' Sergey obviously wanted me to know that there was more to him than driving large trucks.

'When did you get married?' I asked tentatively, wanting to show interest.

Sergey sighed deeply. 'I married the beautiful Anna just after leaving the institute – we were happy for a while.' He paused as if considering this period of happiness. 'Anna was from Pavlovsky Pasad. We were given an apartment in 1991, which was great for a while and gave me a place to finish my thesis.' He glanced over to make sure he had my full attention before continuing. 'The dynamic behaviour and stability of closed cylindrical shells with temperature-sensitive thermo-uneven loading.' Well that was the gist of what he said, which is why I looked at Sergey with no little amount of scepticism – assuming that he was pulling my leg. However, he was being deadly serious and why wouldn't he have been? It turned out to be something to do with nuclear missiles. 'Didn't do me much good,' he added. 'Institutes were closing everywhere and nobody was being paid, so I thought

I'd have a go at retail – selling and reselling anything I could get my hands on, sweets, clothing, shoes, I even bought and then sold a donkey – I made twenty dollars on that donkey.' A brief look of satisfaction arrived on Sergey's face as he considered the profit the donkey had gained him. 'But that wasn't enough and even with Anna's wage as an accountant it was a real struggle. Anna left and I hit the road.'

Eventually conversation dried up and I began to doze. I was awoken what felt like hours later – but can only have been minutes, as the same tune was playing on the stereo – by Sergey prodding me and in turn repeatedly putting his thumb and index finger to his mouth. It was time for a service stop.

We pulled up behind an articulated lorry with Murmansk plates, alongside a shanty kiosk on a slight slant, the size of a toilet cubicle. A fire burned within its shadow and a group of men sat around the fire on logs. The buzz of conversation grew as we approached. I counted Sergey shake five hands, before introducing me as the 'guest'. I shook hands with all present, which amounted to six as the kiosk owner came out from behind his counter, before a particularly short man with a cigarette sizzling between his lips gave up his tree trunk for me. He dismissed all my attempts at refusal with a sharp wave of his back hand, clipping the surface of the wood.

A vessel like a baked-bean can steaming with hot vodka and raspberry preserve was soon offered. I sipped the soothing liquid and passed it on to Sergey, who squatted beside me. He knew everyone; they were all fellow truckers. They spent some time discussing issues of the road – a log spill, traffic cops – before attention turned to me. Yuri, whose trunk I was now perched on, was the first to ask, 'Where are you heading?' I told them about the wedding in Astrakhan. My plans were met with a considered silence before a lanky man in a gold shell suit with sunglasses resting on his head spoke up.

'My first girlfriend came from a town near Astrakhan.' He paused. 'She went to live in America.' He paused again. 'That's why I hate America.' He laughed to himself. 'But not all bad – I married her sister.' He laughed some more and the rest of the group soon joined in.

His was a story to be heard all over Russia, as after the break-up of the Soviet Union throughout the nineties there had been a steady exodus of Russians to the USA. The numbers have been significant but not massive, as often believed. Naturally as the post-Soviet period unravelled, people went in search of better economic opportunities and a sense of stability and security which was fast disappearing in Russia; and specifically the more dynamic Russian women left, leaving an army of bewildered men behind. Russians had been heading to the US en masse for decades, however, so this was nothing new. The first wave was the turn of the twentieth century and coincided with large numbers of other emigrants leaving from Europe – Irish, Scots and Italians included. The second wave came after the 1917 Revolution, the third after the Second World War, and the fourth between 1970 and 1980 (exclusively Jewish Russians). The fifth wave happened from 1991 onwards.

We might think in the West that over the last twenty years most of the Russian populace has in fact packed their bags and moved abroad. However, there has been no shortage of people moving into the Russian Federation. Russia has the second largest stock of migrants in the world with 12 million, after the United States which has 42.8 million. Approximately 9 per cent of its population is foreign-born; Russia is the main destination for migrants within the region of Eurasia.

Yuri cleared his throat and stroked his cheek before telling me, 'I have a friend in Nizhni Novogorod.'

After some more throat clearing he demanded a pen, from nobody in particular. The kiosk owner soon provided one and Yuri wrote a number down on a scrap of paper gathered from his pocket. 'My friend will help you,' he said, passing it to me. After the tin can of liquid had done several more rounds, Sergey nudged me, and we repeated all the handshaking then returned to his lorry, but not before exchanging a few roubles at the kiosk for a tasty shaslyk, which must have been over a foot long. By the time we reached the outskirts of Russia's third largest city I felt completely at ease in Sergey's company, quite at home in the cab and reluctant to have to say another goodbye.

CHAPTER THREE

NO BIKES BUT BEARDS

I called the number on the scrap of paper that had found its way into my pocket, glad to have a contact and a potential way in to the city. Yuri's friend Victor answered within two rings, and told me he was busy that evening but would be happy to meet up with me the following day. He recommended the Hotel Volga, which happened to be close by, and kindly offered to ring ahead for me and book a room at the best price, to save me the trouble and having to pay more as a foreigner. I gratefully accepted his offer.

After a leisurely breakfast of yoghurt, fruit and hard-boiled eggs, I met Yuri's old friend and my new friend Victor in the hotel reception. He was a particularly long and narrow man whose gaze launched itself inquisitively off the end of his pointed nose. He had a big smile, despite looking like he might fall apart at any moment. His most prominent feature was the slab of facial hair attached to his chin, clinging on like a hairy brick. Victor clocked me stealing a prolonged glance and seemed to purr with pride as his hand stroked downwards on his beard.

'Nikolai Bulganin was born in the city.' He paused for any sign of recognition, but I had never heard of Bulganin so offered none. Victor, having the confirmation he needed, continued.

'He was the humble son of an office worker who joined the Bolshevik party in 1917, and in 1918 was recruited into the Cheka. Loyal Stalinist, he was elected into the Communist Party's Central Committee.' He paused again as if to see if he was ringing any bells. He wasn't. 'As others fell victim to the purges, Bulganin progressed rapidly up the ranks. During the war he served as Stalin's principal agent in the Red Army. He was promoted to Marshal of the Soviet Union and became the minister in charge of all the armed forces. He travelled with Khrushchev to Britain (among other countries), where they were known as "the B and K show". Later, during the Suez Crisis he sent letters to Britain and France threatening rocket attacks on London and Paris.' At this point a conspiratorial smile came onto Victor's face and again he stroked his brick. 'So he was quite a guy in the Soviet Union. However, his greatest legacy was the "Bulganin Beard", which indeed mine is modelled on.' Certainly a beard to be proud of... and Victor was. I got the feeling that this was not the first time he had delivered that particular introduction.

Victor clearly preferred to speak with me in high-pitched English rather than suffer my Russian; he didn't say this but the painful expression on his taut face every time I spoke certainly did. Niceties out of the way, it was down to business, and the business Victor was in involved putting Novogorod's best municipal foot forward. If it was the last thing he did, Victor was going to leave a good impression of him and his home town with this particular friend of a friend. We passed from the warmth of the hotel into the crisp air and climbed into his 4x4. 'I will show you around my city and then you will take the bus to Kazan.' I hadn't given my onward travel much consideration. But seeing as I had had more than enough 'free' travel for one journey and Kazan was my next destination, it struck me that the bus would be a pretty good way of getting there. I was still in plenty of time for the wedding, with just under a month to play with, so could afford a few more Olev-style false starts... but not too many.

First stop was the city's main square, Minin Square, positioned in the shadow of the kremlin, on a hill above the Volga. The square was named after Kuzma Minin, who in 1612 brought together the so-called national militia and forced the Polish out of Moscow. In so doing he managed to end the Time of Troubles and establish the rule of the Romanov dynasty. A prosperous local butcher and meat trader, well liked and trusted, it was Minin who was chosen to look after the funds to raise the Second Volunteer Army. He went on to distinguish himself as a skilled soldier – unsurprisingly with his background, he was pretty handy with a sharp blade – and as a result of his combative prowess he was made a nobleman and a member of the Boyar Duma under the new Czar Michael Romanov. He died in 1616 and was interred in the Archangel Cathedral.

***

From the ideally proportioned square we followed a narrow road lined with merchant houses, pale blue and ochre in colour. We came to a halt next to a bronze statue some twenty metres high perched on a cylindrical plinth. The statue was of a man staring wistfully into the distance beyond the river. Victor cleared his throat and lit a cigarette. He then cleared his throat once more whilst gazing at the man with admiration in his eyes.

'Valery Chkalov was the son of a boiler maker – he became a test pilot for aircraft and a "Hero of the Soviet Union".' I nodded my approval, though more at the breathtaking view than the monument. 'His greatest achievement was a non-stop flight of 5,475 miles, taking him 63 hours from Moscow to Vancouver via the North Pole.'

The man on the plinth now had my full attention, as did Victor, who after a long inhale on his cigarette, continued. 'During Chkalov's career in the 1920s and 1930s the Soviet Union glorified its pilots – they were second only to Stalin himself in importance. They weren't seen as a political threat and Chkalov reaped all the benefits of this particular celebration.' Victor's apparent regard for the pilot didn't stop him from stubbing out his cigarette on the base of the plinth, spraying ash into the breeze. 'The village in which he was born is now called Chkalovsk, and from 1938 to 1957 the city of Orenburg in the Urals was called Chkalov. For a while there was a Chkalov Street in Moscow – there is even a Chkalov Drive in Vancouver.'

Victor fumbled around in his pocket for another cigarette, before gently backing away from the 560 steps that led down to the lightly rippling river. 'This is a good place for athletes to train… However, Victor is no athlete.' He laughed, and I laughed too, relieved that we wouldn't be tackling the steps. With a full, toothy smile on his face, Victor pronounced, 'Next I take you to a museum, the money museum.' He was clearly very happy with this particular addition to his tour.

I initially thought he was joking – an ironic Russian take on contemporary culture – but after a short drive in the 4x4 down a leafy street we pulled up outside a wooden house, and above the front door in bold English were the words: 'The Money Museum of Nizhni Novogorod'. It was no joke. As Victor proceeded to thump the door with his clenched fist he told me that the museum had been set up by his friend a couple of years back, and that it had proved very popular with foreign tourists. I was a little doubtful as to how popular the city was with foreign tourists, let alone this museum with its rather curious premise, but I said nothing and followed him in.

It was indeed a whole museum, albeit a small one, dedicated to money – except that admission was free. Cabinets displayed money dating back centuries from all the countries of the old Empire and beyond; Kolkhian tetries dating back to the fourth century BC sat alongside Persian currency, Turkish coins and Polish thalers. This was certainly the best money museum I'd ever visited – although there wasn't much competition. Probably the most prestigious coin on display was the tetradrachm of ancient Colchian money – 'the world's oldest money', or so the description stated next to the treasure. After a short trip down a money lover's memory lane we arrived back in the hallway, where it was possible to buy for not inconsiderable amounts of money copies of the coins and notes that were on display.

Now, Russia isn't short of a church or two, but of all the many churches and cathedrals there is one in particular whose story has intrigued me the most, and that story was told to me by Victor that day in Nizhni Novogorod. Victor had said it was well worth a visit, not least due to speculation that it would soon be pulled down. 'You can't buy what this church can give you,' he had said enthusiastically.

The man responsible for building this particular church was one of many court advisors to the Czar who also just happened to be a particularly skilled sculptor in his spare time. We left the 4x4 at the bottom of a steep hill and began walking, passing a saw mill now rotten and rusted. Around the entrance gate to the church, a colony of beggars had set up camp. I climbed through them to gain entry, whilst Victor skipped off around the back of the building muttering something about 'iconostasis preservation'. Beyond the intricately carved wooden doorway I was hit by a strong smell of damp. The floor appeared to have a light covering of sand, and the walls were decorated with faded mosaics, the most prominent of which was Mary holding in her arms the baby Jesus, who with the crude assistance of the elements seemed to have a larger head than his melancholy-looking mother. By contrast, the bell tower could well have been given a coat of paint minutes before our arrival; all that was missing was the bell. Victor was quick to inform me that in 1991 it had been one of the first churches in the city to be designated for restoration. Work began but the roubles ran out, so work stopped with only the bell tower having been painted.

Two magnificent stained-glass windows got my attention but soon faded into insignificance once I'd caught sight of the marble altar. The original gold hadn't lost its sparkle and the marble retained its cool glow, as pure as the complexion of a child. I was dazzled by a sea-green vaulted roof that appeared to be lightly glowing. Frescoes of saints and angels decorated the walls. I've never been sure about the use made of churches, but I've never been in any doubt about their beauty, and this one was gorgeous.

Victor hadn't entered the church with me, but I hadn't entered the church alone. I sat down close to the altar, and as I did a man half my size with very little hair on his head and a clump on the end of his chin came and sat down next to me. Both his eyes seemed to be closed.

'It is very powerful.'

Well, that's what I think he said. Just as I was about to question his wisdom, he jumped to his feet and left the building. I carried his chilling words with me around the back of the church, where I found Victor chuffing on a cigarette whilst scratching away at a mosaic on the crumbling wall. Seeing me, he stepped back from the wall and declared, 'Time for some refreshments.'

* * *

Victor, who was putting more than a little energy into his 'tour', suggested resting over a coffee at a street-side cafe. A waitress appeared at our table who seemed to know him; they passed a few moments in casual conversation about the new surface of the road, laughing about how the work would never be completed.

The sun was now warm enough to provoke a small trickle of sweat on Victor's brow, which he wiped with his sleeve as he spoke.

'My city is good, no?' Given the circumstances there was only one answer to this question. I had no time to offer it as Victor continued. 'My fee for guiding is very little and as you have come recommended it will be even less – however, I give you a chance to keep your money.' This was the first I'd heard that there was a chance I'd be parting with my money, but by then it came as no surprise. I was beginning to suspect the word for 'free' had been removed from the Russian lexicon. 'I will wrestle you.'

Now this I hadn't been expecting and my face gave away my surprise. Victor seemed to enjoy these few moments before adding, 'I will wrestle you with my arm.' He laughed for the first time since we'd met. I also noticed his tea- and tobacco-stained teeth for the first time. He placed his elbow on the plastic table in expectation of mine joining it. His palm open, a gold wedding band glimmering in the sun, Victor wasn't going to take no for an answer. Now I didn't have my guide down as the combative type and even now, looking closely at his arm, shirt sleeve rolled up above his diminutive bicep, I fancied my chances, for no other reason than my arm was twice the size of his. He seemed completely unperturbed. I even saw a sparkle in his blue eyes that said, 'You have no chance.'

We linked hands and our eyes met across the table. The grip was firm. The waitress had taken a seat in readiness for the role of referee, apparently not for the first time. Just before she gave the go ahead to begin, Victor added, 'If you win, Angliski, you decide how much you pay for my tour.' From that point on, and I think simply because he referred to me as English, it became about so much more than the value of his tour. I was representing my country now; the pride of an entire nation was at stake. My humiliation was rapid, the force of Victor's downward pressure thumping the surface and in turn dislodging a leg from the already unsteady table, cups plummeting to the ground. Victor was calm in victory as if having merely played out an inevitable scenario. I was left with a very sore hand whilst considering how much the pain was going to cost me. We settled on twenty dollars.

***

Despite the early hour – it was just after 5 a.m. – the streets around the Kazan Central train station were throbbing with life. Travellers heading home after long journeys jostled with taxi drivers battling for business. I had just arrived and was somewhat disorientated after several hours on a cramped bus, so quickly found an empty cafe in view of the station building masked by scaffold. The Danny DeVito-lookalike proprietor struggled with a long pole in his attempt to prop up an awning. I drank a coffee served in a thimble-sized cup whilst watching a man in a batik headscarf battle with a holdall twice his size. Forward movement was slow until he eventually gave up, deciding it made a much better seat on which to smoke a cigarette. Once seated, he was quickly approached by a man of oriental appearance who unwittingly (I'm guessing) wore a T-shirt with the wording 'I love young girls' printed on the front. He asked the resting man for a cigarette which was duly proffered.

Kazan had for centuries been a key link in the Volga's mythical evolution and in present-day Russia it was a city on the up: close enough to Moscow to be significant, yet rich in its own identity. The sun warmed the city quickly after its arrival, sometime after my second coffee. Having soaked up the scene from my vantage point, I ambled over to make use of the station 'facilities'. I got a warm smile from the X-ray machine operative before being disarmed by what sounded like a sincerely genuine offer: 'Anything I can help you with?' A friendly official… surely not! I slowly nodded my bemusement back at him, aware that the last time I had asked a Russian official for help he had removed four hundred dollars from my wallet. The station interior seemed to shake with short bursts of very loud military music through speakers positioned at intervals on the high ceiling, suggesting all was well in the USSR. The old woman manning the gents from a bedraggled armchair was very cheerful also. She slapped a wad of tissue into my hand big enough to mummify both me and her, before apologetically requesting the rouble equivalent of £2. I fast realised why everybody was pleased to see me: it wasn't only Tartarstan's oil that was bringing in the wealth.

I planned to find a boat that would take me from Kazan down to Ulyanovsk, roughly 150 kilometres, but first I planned to freshen up in a hotel overnight. Well, that was the plan. The first hotel I tried had no rooms available. I thought nothing of this – it was a May weekend after all. I thought much the same when I got a similar response from the lady with a goldfish expression at the second hotel I visited, next door to the first and only a few hundred metres down the road from the station. I continued my search unperturbed. Kazan is a very straightforward city to navigate, having grown off the river like fungus on a tree trunk. So I headed north away from the Volga and towards the heart of the town. Streets here were quieter than around the station, with the exception of occasional revellers falling out of venues into the early morning. The next hotel, beyond the canal that cut through the city from west to east, was a Hotel Ibis. I couldn't believe my luck as I approached a building seemingly made from glass and looking brand new compared to its ramshackle surrounds. Hotel Ibis had always been the provider of comfortable, reasonably priced rooms, in my experience. It was a little Western-style oasis and I was quite happy to shun local authenticity. I had always turned up at them late without booking and never had availability issues, which was reassuring given my current predicament.

A particularly glamorous couple were at reception to greet me. As I reached the counter they looked me up and down. They took their time, as if letting me build up the maximum levels of hope, before firing in harmony, 'Sorry no rooms!'

This was said in Russian and sounded considerably more brutal than in English. I felt immediately indignant and exclaimed: 'What, you haven't got anything, anything at all?' This time it was personal. Within the walls of this temple of pristine glass and fake teak modernity there must, I concluded, be at least one bed that could be mine for the night. Furthermore, I was fast realising I really did want a bed now. I think my words might have come out a bit louder than is polite, but my agitation was only emphasised by the cool and calm repose maintained by the receptionists. The man, who was clearly enjoying my annoyance, asked, 'Do you have a booking?'

If I had booked, I could have already been in a hot shower, yet because I hadn't possessed the clarity of forethought I was now at the whim of my tormentors. Unfortunately, I had no better response than: 'No.' As I said it I retreated onto the street, leaving the receptionist with a rather smug look of victory on his face, whilst I pondered why there should have been anything to be victorious over.

I continued up through the city's central boulevard running parallel to the murky canal. A couple of dishevelled donkeys, draped in ribbons and led by pre-teen girls in summer dresses, carried children across the paving. The road became steeper as it neared the crest of the hill that Kazan is set on. I had accepted my three hotel rejections with the knowledge that there were some twenty more hotels in the city to choose from. Suddenly, Hotel Tartarstan loomed with all its Soviet menace in front of me. I found myself skipping towards it, striding through the doors and smiling confidently at the middle-aged lady who sat in near darkness on reception. Rather than ask the question I heard myself stating, 'You don't have any rooms available, do you?' I still felt disappointment when she confirmed they didn't. I left quickly, feigning nonchalance, but deep down

I knew that she was thinking, 'If only he'd booked, things could have been so different.'

At the top of the hill was Kremlyovskaya Street. Straight as the flight of an arrow and lined with pretty pastel-coloured townhouses, it ran all the way down to the kremlin. As I approached, it occurred to me that it would have been from within the walls of this brooding structure that the people of Kazan had watched the approach of Pugachev.

WHO WAS PUGACHEV?

Emilian Pugachev was probably the best known of the Cossack bandits that made a name for themselves in the Volga region. In 1773 he began a crusade against the dire conditions of the serfs in Russia. His brigand army primarily attracted criminals and social outcasts of all varieties. However, his cause also galvanised real discontents, particularly among the Bashkirs, Tartars, and Kalmyks from the southern Volga. As his army quickly grew to an impressive 30,000 in number, Pugachev became the greatest threat to domestic stability during Catherine the Great's entire reign. He even claimed to be Catherine's murdered husband Peter III, although this was unlikely and certainly never proved.

In the summer of 1774, having won a battle with the Russian army, Pugachev crossed the River Kama and entered Kazan to have a quick look around. Having been previously imprisoned in the city it was believed he bore a special grudge against Kazan. It was a feeling with which I was beginning to empathise. The next day,

Pugachev and his men returned to the city disguised as women and set fire to the kremlin. Kazan lost as many as 2,000 houses and a number of priests were slaughtered in their churches. I wasn't going to butcher any priests, although I might have had more luck finding a hotel room by employing some of Pugachev's chicanery.

Russia's national poet, Alexander Pushkin, was so interested in the legend that was Pugachev that he not only studied all the available archive material, but also visited the governorates that had taken part in the rebellion and spoke to eyewitnesses. He went on to write *The History of Pugachev* and his story 'The Captain's Daughter' is also about the Cossack pretender.

I followed Kremlyovskaya Street until tempted by a rotting bench in a pocket-sized, dishevelled park in front of the cream-painted university building. On the rotting bench opposite were a young couple in an advanced state of embrace. I didn't notice them until I was seated and it was very difficult not to stare. The male contingent of the 'love-in' caught my gaze and smiled before resuming his activity with even more enthusiasm. I recalled a notable German professor of Kazan University, Karl Fuchs, who carried out experiments with Tartar women in the eighteenth century. He bizarrely liked to make them fall in love with him and then when he withdrew his affection he studied the quality of their unhappiness. He died alone and miserable.

Kazan was one of seven major universities in Russia at the time and, unlike many of the others, was politically fairly sleepy until as late as the 1890s, dominated by German professors as in much of Russia, rather than political firebrands. Beyond the questionable study of ethnography, science and mathematics were the subjects that flourished at Kazan University. Gorky once said of a mathematician with whom he shared a flat in the city, 'Geometry's a cage, yes! A mousetrap! A prison!' This was about as heated as the scholars got in the city until the 1890s, at which point the grey cells were usurped by the potent energies of revolution. Lenin's father was a Kazan mathematician who later followed the Volga south from Kazan (as I would) to become a teacher in Astrakhan.

Some Kazan students of the mid-nineteenth century did become famous – although as no direct result of having attended the university. In 1844 Leo Tolstoy enrolled as a student of oriental languages; within a year he had failed his exams, switched to law and lost his virginity to a prostitute. It took him another couple of years to realise the secret of his success was not to be the influence of textbooks but that of other great writers, at which point he packed his bags and returned to Yasnaya Polyana, near Tula just south of Moscow. Here he would spend the rest of his life being rather eccentric and arguably one of the greatest writers who ever lived.

Forty years after Tolstoy had packed his bags Lenin arrived, only to be expelled after only four months of studying law, accused of taking part in a demonstration. It's doubtful whether he was actually guilty as charged; however, his cause wasn't helped by the recent execution of his revolutionary brother for a bungled attempt on the life of the reactionary Czar Alexander III. Like Tolstoy, having withdrawn from the world of institutions, Lenin was able to work alone and truly become himself.

The third memorable person with strong links to Kazan University was Maxim Gorky; although, as he didn't actually set foot in a lecture theatre, perhaps he doesn't count. He arrived in the city in 1884 with every ambition of improving his life, but due to lack of formal qualifications he was prevented from enrolling for studies. Most of his life he was plagued by his status as self-educated, not least because he didn't feel at home with intellectuals anyway. He ended up working in a bakery in Kazan. This later provided much material for his book *Twenty-Six Men and a Girl*, which amongst other things was about the brutality of Russian life.

Gorky had had a miserable, loveless childhood which resulted in him, at the age of nineteen, attempting to take his own life. On the banks of the Kazanka beneath the kremlin wall, he shot himself, aiming for the heart. He missed, and instead permanently damaged his lungs. Whilst in hospital he tried a second time by drinking acid. His suicide note was passed over to the Blagoveshchensky Church, who called him in for a telling off; he told them, 'Next time I'll hang myself from your gates.'

Gorky was so bored by Kazan that he taught himself to play the violin. Lenin, also very bored by Kazan, played a lot of chess. Gorky was well aware of the effects of boredom on the Russian character, having written, in his book *Childhood*:

To Russians, through the poverty and squalor of their lives, suffering comes as a diversion, is turned into a game and they play it like children and rarely

feel ashamed of their misfortune. In the monotony of
everyday existence grief comes as a holiday and a fire is
an entertainment. A scratch embellishes an empty face.

I wasn't going to take any chances with boredom myself, so got busy once more searching for a bed.

At the bottom end of the road stood the intimidating Soviet megalith, Hotel Kazan. I passed through a market on my way there. It was an airy white-tiled hall bustling with colour, sporting produce from all over the ex-Soviet Union, melons from Uzbekistan and tomatoes from Georgia. Dark-skinned vendors harangued passers-by, thrusting fresh fruit on the tips of sharp blades into people's faces. Ladies ladled *smetana* (a thick sour cream); pickled cucumbers sat alongside mounds of stout garlic balls.

The entrance to the hotel comprised a souvenir shop selling all sorts of tat: matryoshka dolls, shell suits with 'Russia' emblazoned on them, scarves, *palekh* spoons and boxes designed in a region of the same name north of Moscow, and more. I was quickly cornered by a security guard who displayed the reluctant enthusiasm of a man who had clearly been on duty all night with very little to do. I provided him with a real opportunity to justify his meagre salary. I'd already thought I'd try a less direct approach at this establishment and try to humour my adversaries before going in for the kill. 'Busy night?' I duly began.

The man had no hair but began stroking his scalp as if he had. He smelt of tobacco and sure enough reached for a cigarette as if the smoke was necessary to lubricate his voice box. After a deep inhalation he simply said, 'What?' After such a drawn-out build-up I had rather hoped he was going to be more interesting.

He obviously believed my opening gambit and attempt at petty and pointless civil conversation to be as daft and wholly un-Russian as I did. His enquiry could have been somewhat ambiguous: what did I want, what was I doing, what was my business, what did I mean? However, after years of hearing Russians brusquely grunting this one-syllable world of possibilities at me, I knew exactly what he was getting at and on this occasion was quick to narrow it down to its purest Slavic form: 'Sod off and leave me alone to do bugger all, then I can go home and do some more of the same…'

I swerved past the doorman and made my way over to a very long reception counter. Displaying my humblest countenance I asked the woman, who was doing a good job of pretending to be busy, if she might take pity on me and give me a very expensive, grotty little room (I kept to myself the description of the room I would have happily settled for at that stage). I quickly pointed out that the extortionate price she would no doubt charge me for being a foreigner was not a problem. 'No rooms,' she said, without raising her head from the blank page she seemed to be reading.

It was time for breakfast. Relegating the idea of a warm shower to the back of my mind, I ventured into the first porta-cabin cafe I came to; the Pepsi sign hanging precariously from the branch of a tree outside gave it away. The short dark-skinned man behind the counter smiled at me as I entered. He then went so far as to ask me how I was. Now, I thought, this man was either a local after my money or not a local at all.

It turned out he was from Uzbekistan. He had been in the city three years and business was going well. He asked me where I was from, where I was going, how many children I had and where my wife was. A number of other personal questions followed, the appropriateness of which seemed uncertain at nine o'clock in the morning.

However, he was the friendliest person I had encountered in the city, so I was happy for him to ask me anything. I enjoyed a lovely cup of Nescafe 3-in-1 and three potato pancakes. Back out onto the street I felt re-invigorated after half an hour spent in the company of that gentle and very inquisitive man, who found himself a long way from his native Tashkent. I was now armed not only with a full stomach but also the names of three more hotels I had yet to try. However, I wasn't very hopeful.

The road I was on led directly to the ferry port, so I quickly nurtured Plan B.

PLAN B:

Forgo shower, bed and any other pleasures that come with a hotel room and take a boat the 150 kilometres down river to Ulyanovsk.

I had, of course, hoped to stay longer than six hours in the Tartar capital. I just wasn't in the mood for any more rejection. As I approached the ferry terminal building, I passed a crowd gathering outside the bus station laden with stripy holdalls and bin liners. From a distance the terminal was impressive: shards of blue-tinted glass glistened in the sunlight. Closer inspection, however, revealed a different story, like kissing a beautiful princess only for her to transform before your very eyes into an ugly, old witch.

The building was not only closed; it appeared to have not been open for some time. It was worn and forlorn, the grand design suggesting vast ambitions that had become redundant. Staring through the dusty heavy windows, I saw it had been decked out in high spec. Many of the office units were empty of furniture and the carpet was damp and had been devoured by mould. I rattled a few doors in an attempt to gain entry but all were locked – quite unnecessarily, as several glass panels had been removed wholesale, making it possible to simply step inside should anyone wish.

At the riverfront a fleet of fishing boats bobbed up and down, tightly nestled together along a wooden-slat jetty. Much to my delight there were also cruisers and pleasure boats in varying degrees of disrepair. I asked a fisherman to recommend a boat for me to take on my journey south. He chuckled and said, 'Better for you to walk,' gesturing upriver. As I looked closer at the collection of shabby craft, I realised he may have had a point.

The temporary-looking ticket office for pleasure boats was hidden behind a line of trees which effected complete dissociation with the now pointless terminal building. Inside the usual scrum was taking place that seems to occur anywhere in Russia where it is possible to purchase a ticket (or anywhere it is possible to part with money... oddly). It doesn't matter what the ticket will allow you to do once bought; potential buyers become crazed, wild, their eyes bloodshot and maniacal. I fast sensed that until I too had crossed the line and shed many layers of common humanity it would be impossible to get my hands on the ticket I needed for Plan B and the passenger boat to Ulyanovsk. In fact it was impossible to get into a position close enough to the purveyor behind the glass to even begin negotiations.

Just the thought of having to buy a ticket in Russia induced an anxiety in me. This particular ticket office possessed an added layer of discomfort in that there was an evident atmosphere of frivolity, as was to be expected with the prospect of a jolly trip down the river. Whole families oozed about as one amoeba-like, space-grabbing organism. The place was chaotic, indecipherable, but worst of all the atmosphere was joyous – everybody was full of the excitement at the expectation of pleasure – which somehow, for me, made the situation even more unpleasant.

After an hour of being mauled, grappled and shrieked at in a fashion that would have given rise to criminal charges in the civilised West, I got my ticket and was ejected from the cramped ticket office like a ball from a cannon. With two hours to kill before departure on the good ship *Sable*, I collected myself, stocked up on refreshment and looked forward to the prospect of actually being afloat on the Volga once again.

CHAPTER FOUR

ALL ABOARD FOR ULYANOVSK

'I could have gone on flying through space forever.'
Yuri Gagarin

The good ship *Sable* was less of a ship and more of a floating capsule – spacious she wasn't. At approximately thirty feet in length, she had most of that length taken up by the cockpit, and the passenger area appeared to have been squeezed in as an afterthought. As I climbed on board, any vision I'd been harbouring of spending six hours gliding down the river on deck disappeared as swiftly as the daylight. The windows were all heavily tinted, making it difficult to see out and greatly reducing the natural light inside the cabin, while even to look through them required an unnatural craning of the neck since the limited space between seats made it necessary to sit bolt upright. This wasn't comfortable. I sat down reluctantly, accepting that I'd be staring at the cushioned insulation panels for the rest of the journey.

There was, however, some consolation to be travelling downriver in a capsule as opposed to one of the more traditional boats that cruised the route from Kazan to Ulyanovsk. Only months earlier, a 50-year-old tourist ferry went down with 188 passengers. The *Bulgaria*, built in 1955 in Czechoslovakia, sank so quickly there was only time to launch two lifeboats before it plunged to the bottom of the 20-metre-deep Kuibyshev reservoir. Two passing ships didn't stop to help. The ship had been travelling from Bulgar to Kazan along a stretch of the river that is in parts 19 miles wide. Russia's Union of the Tourism Industry said that the ship hadn't been inspected for years, and their spokesman had concluded unsympathetically that the ship had 'deserved to sink'.

Minutes before the scheduled departure time I was joined by a family of three, two middle-aged parents and a teenage daughter. Despite there being nine seats left, the mother quickly informed me that I was in her seat, and by way of emphasis she thrust her ticket in my face. There was no argument from me. I ripped my bag out from whence I'd stuffed it and shuffled over to one of the many remaining seats.

Russians possess a well-disguised code of obedience: they will fight their way onto a bus/train/boat/aeroplane as if the last loaf of bread on the planet is on board and then calmly demand the seat that has been reserved by their ticket. Possibly, because life is so chaotic for them, there exists a fear of anarchy beyond a certain point. Control of sorts is very much required wherever control can be maintained.

Perhaps this fits into Pashukanis's belief about the achievement (or not) of Communism. Pashukanis was a Soviet legal expert best known for his work named *The General Theory of Law and Marxism*. He believed that once Communism had been fully implemented, the law and the state would simply wither away, leaving morality, as we understand it, with no function, making way for a perverse, contradictory breed of order. If my new travelling companions were anything to go by, I think the writer's theory may have been correct.

Suddenly there was a rush for the gangplank, causing the *Sable* to rock from side to side. Passengers of all shapes and sizes bundled their way onto the vessel and, in so doing, pushed the waterline up several feet. Deciding consequently that it might be prudent to settle myself in my allotted seat, I moved to the somewhat isolated seat number ten, which happened to be the only one facing backwards. On the bright side, it afforded me perhaps more leg room, as I was able to swing them to one side, and furthermore I'd been told that facing backwards was the safest way to travel. On the darker side, however, due to the build-up of luggage all around me, if I so much as moved any part of my body above the waist I was more than likely to get involved in an inappropriate violation of the person facing me, whom I was now centimetres away from. For better or worse, I had bought a ticket that would take me down the river backwards.

With the roar of the engine, we pulled away from the jetty and all eighteen pairs of eyes were on me as I was at the front of the boat and the only person facing backwards. I appeared to be the only distraction, as it was too noisy to chat and, due to the angles involved, looking out the window called for the flexibility of a contortionist. I would have hidden my discomfort by looking out of the window, except that bending my head the necessary inches to see out of the window would have required me to plant it within the cleavage of the lady opposite. It could have been a satisfactory space-saving solution if my gaze wasn't being heavily monitored by a bull of a man sitting next to her, who I assumed had more than a passing interest in said lady's chest. It was too late for recriminations. I was stuck, unable to move, with nine Russians staring at me, for another six hours. And just when I thought things couldn't get any worse, they did.

The boat pulled up alongside a jetty two kilometres upriver from Kazan, and the door opened allowing the sun to burst in. If I could have moved I would have exited the boat there and then, but I couldn't move – I had become an unwilling captive on a boat down the Volga. With mounting horror I witnessed four more passengers climb aboard. Surely, I thought, there wouldn't be enough oxygen for everybody. As the newcomers jammed themselves into non-existent spaces, I thought of the insight shown by the woman who had previously demanded her seat; this was a perfect free-for-all; this was pleasure cruising Russian-style. Yet it dawned on me that this was never meant to be a pleasure cruise for anyone but myself; this was whole families taking all their belongings and entire family to Ulyanovsk as an alternative to the bus. What, I wondered, was wrong with the train?

I had always been taught that it was rude to stare, but there were very few places to put my gaze without it landing on somebody's face. Thus I worked my way around the collected faces on the boat, trying not to spend more than a few seconds on each. Occasionally I would be caught and eye contact was made – then a fleeting game of chicken would ensue, to see who would hold the other's gaze the longest. As the journey progressed I grew in confidence and by the time we'd reached Bulgar I had managed to convince myself that I was indeed sitting in the champion's seat rather than the dunce's chair. If nothing else, I knew the features of my fellow passengers pretty well and would have made a perfect identity-parade witness, although I doubted crime was on anybody's mind after this voyage – several days of recovery perhaps, outstretched on a comfortable bed, but nothing more strenuous.

As it was, the scheduled stop at the picturesque settlement of Veliky Bulgar couldn't have come quickly enough. After being cooped up for four and a half hours, I had lost all feeling in every part of my body, my legs unable to carry me until full circulation had returned. The ancient village not only offered the opportunity for some much-needed leg-stretching; it very nearly made the discomfort of the previous hours worthwhile. It was at its best in the sunshine, oozing bygone Russia, the likes of which I had been starved of for some time.

'I came to visit a sacred town with permission of Sahibs
What a wonderful place that town seemed to me...'
Unknown poet, writing about Bulgar

Veliky Bulgar is a ruined town on the high left bank of the Volga, approximately 140 kilometres from Kazan. It was once the homeland of the mighty Bulgars, ancestors of today's Tartars. It is now a place of pilgrimage. In 922, Islam was embraced in the town after the visit of an ambassador from Baghdad. Then in 1236 the town was demolished, becoming part of the Golden Horde. This was a Mongol and later Turkicized khanate resulting from the Mongol invasions of the thirteenth century. Volga Bulgaria for much of this period was the centre of the fur trade in Eurasia and, as such, very attractive to invading armies.

We walked as a group, I and the other passengers, up to the thirteenth-century cathedral mosque resplendent with its 24-metre minaret, of which another unknown poet wrote:

> *Like a sanctity of our belief*
> *You are standing here, my mosque,*
> *in the crossroads of the ages.*
> *I hear your azan voice from your*
> *high and beautiful minarets.*

Made of white limestone, the mosque sat dominant on a hill. Sunlight flooded into its meeting hall. In front of the main entrance was the northern mausoleum; it was here that the Bulgar nobility took their last refuge, before the arrival of the Mongol armies, who proceeded to destroy the graves. Moving in a stuttering zombie-like procession – in silence as talk was forbidden out of respect for the ancestors – my companions and I passed through an archway into an inner room. Small lancet windows revealed scriptures made by an unknown Bulgar artist. It felt strange to be in this place with the same people I'd been tucked up on the boat with. Now that they all had fully functioning bodies and were away from the context of the boat, they seemed like different people to the ones I had previously been faced with. We had gone from being squeezed together in a boat to being squeezed into a mosque, but at least now there were other things to look at besides each other.

Back in the bright afternoon I wandered towards the rest of the town. Veliky Bulgar had been well developed: archaeologists have found remnants of water systems which would have supplied fountains, houses and bath houses. Five bath houses in all have been found – they would have been important social meeting places for women, with some baths lasting all day. The remnants of three of the bath houses were still visible; concrete mounds some two metres in diameter, worn smooth over the centuries by the elements, would likely have been the bathing pools. Towards the southern part of the village stood another limestone mausoleum. It was a pretty little sanctuary capable of accommodating three or four fully grown adults. I poked my head through the doorway; pigeons purred in a nest in the rafters and a mangy dog lay curled up in the corner. Afterwards, having walked the perimeter of the town, I arrived back at the river to find my fellow passengers re-boarding. It was time to go.

AN IMPORTANT BULGAR

Qol Ghali was a poet and holds the esteemed title of being the founder of medieval Tartar literature. His most famous poem is called *Tale of Yusuf*, believed to have been written in 1233. It is about the struggle against evil and the fight for human happiness. The poem played a massive part in Muslim Volga Bulgar culture and then later in Tartar culture. Inspired by Qur'anic stories of Joseph, it was printed for the first time in 1839 by Raxmatulla Amirxanov. Yusuf or Joseph is a character taken from the Christian bible and was the eleventh son of Jacob, the only one to have been given the gift of prophecy. Trouble started when Joseph had a dream, which his father interpreted to mean that Joseph would become very important one day. Joseph's eleven brothers weren't very happy about this and their jealousy led them to throw Joseph unceremoniously down a well, claiming that he had been attacked and killed by a wolf. However, Joseph is eventually saved from the well and goes on to be a famous interpreter of dreams for the king of Egypt. Andrew Lloyd Webber turned the story into a successful West End musical.

It was getting dark when we pulled into the port at Ulyanovsk. I had been given the name of Hotel Venets and been told that it was near impossible not to find. I usually enjoy arriving in a new town under the cover of darkness, only for it to reveal its true identity in the new light of day; nonetheless I was glad of the ticket collector on the tram that I caught from the river station, who reassured me that she would let me know when to get off. This friendly babushka was the perfect tonic after the boat ride, warm and interested in me and, what's more, eager to be of assistance. She left me with a good feeling about Ulyanovsk which was only to be bolstered during my stay in the city.

Located in the town centre, Ulyanovsk's tallest building, the 42-floor Hotel Venets, had indeed been impossible to miss. As I walked in, I was greeted in English by a cheerful receptionist, who with the minimum of hassle had quickly dispatched me to a very comfortable room. I stared out of my twenty-second-floor window at the distant Volga, lit up by the city lights, a little nervous of going to bed in the fear that I would never wake up. I showered and lay upon the bed and, as is always the way, the discomfort of the past few days became a distant memory; the minute you're on the bus you forget about the long wait in the rain. I was certainly now on my very dry bus.

After a deep and long sleep I awoke eager to explore, like a child at Christmas, keen to unwrap this new city that I had in front of me. I was determined to enjoy it slowly rather than rip the paper off and then impatiently go looking for something else to open. I was making good time for reaching Astrakhan, and due to my unexpectedly brief stay in Kazan I had some time to spare. It was a Sunday so I was not surprised that the streets were empty except for the odd person scurrying along. A gentle breeze blew off the river, offering relief from the already warm sun. Already, in my first moments in Ulyanovsk, I sensed a civic pride that had been glaringly absent in Kazan.

This was emphasised by a poster board on which were some twenty photographs of some very ordinary looking men and women, most of whom were dressed in grey suits. Above the pictures were the words 'Best People of the Town'. A part of me found this display heart-warming and I considered how great it must feel to be one of those people with your picture mounted for all to see: an ongoing pat on the back. Despite the hint of Big Brother lurking in the gesture, it's always nice to be told that you're great. Moreover, the tactic obviously worked; the breezy, tree-lined, attractive streets of Ulyanovsk were spotlessly clean, the result of road sweepers furiously persisting with the help of the wind.

I sat alone in a cafe overlooking the river. Tankers were mere specks in the distance on a shimmering Volga ocean that stretched to the horizon. Could this, I wondered, really be a river? The cafe hadn't yet been reconstructed after the night before, chairs and even a table appearing quite naturally to be resting on their sides. A young girl busied herself tidying and setting up for the day. I took the opportunity to send some texts back home to the UK and sent one to Vicky confirming that I was well on my way. I got an immediate reply:

Me: Am at Ulyanovsk hope still getting married.
V: Wedding off... Dmitry bastard!

There was a long pause whilst I fiddled with my phone, bought another coffee and considered the long trip home.

V: Ha ha got ya! Yeah still getting married, really excited can't wait to see you.

Dmitry was certainly not a bastard, I knew that – he adored Vicky. However, it hadn't always been a smooth ride.

There had been a few obstacles thrown into their road to happiness, fused with their unfair share of bad luck too. Initially the geographical distance between them had taken its toll, which had made the time they did spend together in the early days all the more special.

After the disappointment of their weekend in Paris, Dmitry tried again with a holiday to Tuscany. They had stayed in a pretty Tuscan villa on the side of a hill with views out over the mountains and with smells and colours that were intoxicating. Unfortunately, no amount of intoxication had been enough to get the holiday back on track. The Tuscan holiday hadn't started well. Despite Dmitry's attempts to make sure all arrangements had been double-checked, they still arrived at the check-in desk of their EasyJet flight to Florence to be told by a suitably defensive operative that 'unfortunately' there was no space left on the plane for them (apparently, low-cost airlines have a policy of overbooking flights during the busy summer months). With these words Dmitry entered a phase of incredulous indignation: 'No that can't be right, surely. We've bought tickets and have reserved seats – priority boarding no less, please just check again and you'll quickly see the error of your ways.' When the operative said there had been no mistake and his overall demeanour took on a more combative appearance, the blood from Dmitry's entire body flooded to his head at what could only have been an unhealthy rate. 'Of course we've got seats... now just check us in and we can start the holiday I badly need to seal the deal with this woman I've fallen madly in love with.' Dmitry didn't say the last part, but that's what he was thinking.

With these early signs that he was fast turning into a disgruntled airport holidaymaker cliché, Vicky took the reins, with a calm, methodical approach that adversity had time and time again aroused in her. The result, however, was the same – as they were gestured over to another queue at another counter, where they would be able to get seats on the next flight. Much to Vicky's chagrin and Dmitry's despair, the next flight to Florence wasn't for another three days and their brochure-perfect villa was only booked for a week. Vicky eventually settled for a flight leaving the following day to Rome – I say Vicky, as by this point Dmitry had entered shock, which had been accompanied by a particularly brutal strain of Tourette's, from which nobody was safe. Fortunately, it was Russian Tourette's so nobody was the slightest bit aware that they weren't safe – but merely offered glances of sympathy.

Thus the first night of the holiday was spent at a hotel within the less-than-picturesque surrounds of Gatwick Airport, whilst not on the phone to Phil from EasyJet customer services, downing large quantities of wine in an attempt to help quash the disappointment. They could have just thrown in the towel there and then, but no, that simply wasn't Vicky or Dmitry's style; neither were prepared to just give up. When they eventually arrived in Rome, they cleared the outskirts of the Italian capital heading north in their Seat hire car, only to get a puncture. Now what are the chances of that? This was a question that crashed through Dmitry's head as he changed the wheel by the side of a very busy Italian motorway.

***

I walked back through the centre of Ulyanovsk just as people were beginning to drag themselves out onto the streets. As the town woke, it didn't take long for the muffled sound of techno to start rising in the distance. I found a park with colourful flower beds where, to my relief, the techno was replaced by the music from the film *Titanic* – it fitted the scene perfectly. The park's centrepiece fountain sprung into life with my arrival as if somebody had been on lookout. 'Quick, punter! Cue music and water feature.' I couldn't help but be impressed.

As I fiddled with my camera whilst sitting on a bench, a girl brought her scrawny horse up to the fountain to drink. It was reluctant. 'You can take a horse to water,' I thought, looking on. Finally, however, having plunged its muzzle in and out of the water several times like an elephant at a watering hole, and splashing the girl from top to bottom, suddenly most of the animal's long head vanished into the water and it guzzled furiously, occasionally coming up to snort with pleasure. I watched as the girl led the horse away from the fountain, weaving past the flowers before they both disappeared into the morning.

I hadn't been in the park twenty minutes when the calm morning scene was shattered by the arrival of a legion of army cadets taking photos of one another. They snapped away like Japanese tourists on London Bridge, making full use of the breathtaking backdrop of the river below us. As the sun rose higher, the cadets gradually dissipated, to be replaced by Sunday morning promenaders. Soon there were families everywhere, which only emphasised my solitude, although I still had the river, I thought, and she was very beautiful when she made the effort. Blankets of writhing silver light shimmered on the surface, magical contortions governed by the moon. Standing up, I left my bench and wandered along the promenade through unkempt gardens with the word 'Lenin' sculpted into the grass. A line of empty cafes was coming to life, all carrying a strong sense of hangover from the night before. Having walked a lot, sat a lot, watched a lot, I felt I was getting to know the city. It was time for some lunch.

TWO FACTS ABOUT ULYANOVSK THAT MIGHT BE OF INTEREST

- The city has two rivers running through it: the Volga and the Sviyaga. That they flow in opposite directions gives Ulyanovsk its special creative energy... apparently.
- Eldar Ryazanov's comedy *The Adventures of Italians in Russia* was filmed at the airport... there were no Italians in the cast.

The top floor of the Hotel Venets was occupied by one of its two restaurants, which operated under the name of 'Restoran Easy'. With the prospect of a mouth-watering view I took the shuddering elevator all the way up. Restoran Easy was packed with people eating and drinking, all enjoying the sun and the wonderful views across the city. With my entrance all activity appeared to freeze, except for a handful of black-and-white-dressed staff who simply ignored me. The diners then continued dining and the staff continued to service them. It was left to me to conclude the place was full and that I'd have to forgo the delightful views. I settled for 'Restoran 2', located, more modestly, on the second floor.

Restoran 2 was blessed with open-deck seating which gave ample opportunity to take in the sights and sounds from the street below. Upbeat pop music wafted through the air, along with the sound of men arguing in the distance. From the seductive wooden menu I chose one of the six pasta dishes on offer, the Pasta Mediterranean, only to be told by the waitress, who spoke very softly, that I would have to have the pasta with fish. As I wanted a hearty meal and not a frustrating debate on the integrity of the finely sculpted menu, pasta with fish it was. In the event it wasn't great, but that didn't matter as the ambience of the place more than made up for it. Indeed, the woman could have put a plate down in front of me stacked high with soil from the flower beds and in that place, at that time, I wouldn't have been bothered.

* * *

The Hotel Venets lay a stone's throw from the Lenin Memorial, built to remember the city's most famous son. The legs of the sprawling, seventies sci-fi-style memorial, a starkly Soviet edifice, straddled a pair of houses lived in by the Ulyanovsk family, who would go down in history as the Lenins. Just beyond the two imprisoned houses stood another pretty, grey wooden-slat house which had also been a one-time residence of the Ulyanovsks and was now harbouring a museum.

The lady taking admissions asked me for 20 roubles, then looked at me again and, after asking where I was from, bucked the admission up to 200 roubles. I was passed into the hands of an out-of-breath babushka who proceeded to give me a gasping commentary, as I followed the manuscripts and photographs around the lovely, bright, sunny room.

'There is his father.' She pointed to a sepia print hanging on the wall. 'Fourth child of parents in Astrakhan. Ilya's father,' she spoke as if she had been very close to Ilya, 'was a poor tailor of Tartar or Kalmyk descent. Vladimir was the third child; he had an older brother and sister. His father died when he was sixteen, and shortly afterwards he renounced his belief in God.'

She certainly didn't mince her words. The walls were crammed with old pictures, family portrait after family portrait. I found it amazing that the father of the Soviet state had the time to study Marx; he always seemed to be posing for a photograph. The pictures revealed a close-knit family. Thus the death of both his brother and father around the same time must have impacted greatly on him. Up on the second floor there was no gasping babushka to show me around, but a considerably more smouldering proposition, menacing and intimidating, who largely ignored me and left me to absorb the rest of the exhibits alone.

Lenin's birthplace was originally called Simbirsk. Born into a middle-class family in 1870, he gained an interest in revolutionary leftist politics when his brother was executed in 1887. He quickly dedicated his time to studying law and radical Marxist politics. In 1893 he moved to St Petersburg, where he became a senior figure in 'the League of Struggle for the Emancipation of the Working Class'. Arrested and exiled to Siberia for three years, on completion of his sentence he left Russia, travelling to Western Europe, living in Germany, England and Switzerland, eventually returning home after the February Revolution of 1917.

Subsequently, Lenin took a senior role in orchestrating the October Revolution, as the leader of the Bolsheviks, and thus the establishment of the Russian Socialist Federative Soviet Republic – the world's first constitutionally socialist state. As an intellectual, Lenin developed Marxism and added a Russian application to it which spawned Marxist–Leninist theory, which amongst other things emphasised the role of a political vanguard in the revolutionary process.

Lenin remains a controversial figure. His critics have labelled him a dictator who oversaw considerable abuse of human rights. To his supporters he was a champion, a hero of the working class. Either way, worldwide there are more statues commemorating him than any other person who ever lived.

At one point the 'guide', who had remained silent until then, couldn't help herself and found the need to tell me that a photograph I was looking at was a police photograph, which is why Lenin was looking a bit pale and not at his best. To be honest I had never much considered what constituted a good Lenin photograph, but this apparently wasn't one. Upon closer inspection, however, I was inclined to agree with her – the man in the picture looked like no other I'd seen; among other things, he appeared to have already been embalmed.

The babushka then let loose with a rapid volley in Russian that I found completely incomprehensible but, as I got the impression that this was indeed her intention, I pretended to follow only to give myself away by nodding inappropriately.

Finally the woman offered me a very throaty goodbye, which revealed a penchant for strong tobacco, together with a smirk that indicated she had seen me for the unworthy Western tourist that I was.

I lingered on, soaking up the atmosphere. Along with the photographs, there was other memorabilia. The upstairs rooms had been kept as they were when Lenin lived in them; there was a grand piano, chairs and a room for the kids. The rooms were airy and light, with fine views of the river. As I looked out through the windows I thought what a truly lovely place it must have been to live in, replete with natural beauty and all the trappings of a solid, educated middle-class life in nineteenth-century Russia.

***

My one obligation whilst in Ulyanovsk was to look up an old friend of Dmitry's who ran a school in the city. He had told me that my services were required as a 'native tongue examiner' – a task which, obscure as it was, I felt far from equal to, yet was curious to explore. So on my second day, having completed all Lenin-related activities, I set out to do just that. Svetlana greeted me with a wave of excitement and the declaration: 'Your native English tongue is most welcome in Ulyanovsk.'

A short way from the bus station we crossed a small park sprinkled with neat, mathematically aligned flower beds, then walked along a narrow street by the banks of the river, lined on the opposite side by a tall and battered industrial frontage that blocked out the sun.

From a distance, the building we walked towards could have been mistaken for an imperial home from a former era. Columns framed large blue doors; gold leaf decorated arched windows. The edifice was square in shape, with what appeared to be a crenellated roof – a pocket-sized castle. However, as we came closer, I saw that the windows were cracked and, in places, completely smashed. Bonfires had left large black stains on the worn, cracked steps. The doors were simple sheets of MDF painted blue, the paint now peeled and cracked. My heart went out to this poor, long-neglected building.

Svetlana led me to a door at the side of the building, tightly fastened with rope. 'It never stops people getting in and starting fires,' she said, 'but it makes me feel like I'm trying to protect the place.' On passing through the door, my heart sank. Svetlana, sensing this, tried to refloat it. 'It's as simple as working from one end to the other,' she said, indicating the end where work had begun, although, to be honest, I found it hard to tell.

'One of the biggest problems is keeping the vandals out. We started about three years ago, but we have to stop occasionally and things deteriorate and it's like starting again. It's eventually going to be the new schoolhouse. Meanwhile the council have condemned the building, which is another complication. We really have to fight them to keep work moving forward.'

I thought of Dmitry's rapidly expanding empire and what he would make of such a scheme. I was sure that he would want to help, but not so sure he would have the patience to negotiate all the obstacles being put in the way. An air of resignation crept into Svetlana's voice, matching the surroundings. Planks of wood, splintered and warped, lay strewn about. Large holes in the floor made it all but useless. Chairs decorated the space: some balanced unconvincingly on top of others; others were bizarrely skinned of their soft coating, the wooden frame laid bare. I watched as Svetlana began to right chairs that had been knocked over. I then looked at the hazardous mess of wires, metal poles and wood still tangled together. The building would, I sensed, make a wonderful school, but I wasn't convinced she would see it in her lifetime.

'A little bit more work and it won't be long before, what you say, "All systems go",' she said. Svetlana's enthusiasm was infectious yet I couldn't help feeling that the most sensible course of action would be complete demolition, making room for the arrival of a philanthropic, education-loving businessman to finance the rebuilding. Leaving the project behind us for now, we walked around the corner to her fully functioning existing schoolhouse, complete with a class full of students waiting for a thorough native-tongue examination.

The school building was straight out of the 1950s with wood-panelled walls and high, echoing ceilings. As I entered the classroom, an assembly of stony-faced students rose to their feet and, on Svetlana's introduction, began clapping furiously as if all were connected to a switch. Once the class was settled, Svetlana gave me the floor so I might introduce myself. Observing the expectant collective look on the faces of my audience, I felt that, more than anything else, I had been given the opportunity to explain myself and I immediately began by justifying my travels in Russia. The more I said, the better I realised that it was a good opportunity for me to evaluate, off the cuff, what I was in fact doing on this journey. I talked about the idea of revisiting and observing change; then, realising after a while what a mess I was making of it all, I simply declared, 'The truth is I'm just popping down to Astrakhan for a mate's wedding!'

I was then handed a sheet of paper with approximately five hundred words of small-printed text. My job was to read it out at a 'normal' speed, with clear pronunciation and punctuation. Well, that seemed easy enough, until in the very first sentence I came across a word I had never encountered before and certainly had no idea how to pronounce. I waded on, until having finished the first paragraph I realised that what I had read made no sense at all. The text had clearly been translated word for word into English from Russian using a rather large dictionary, and the result, unfortunately, was gibberish.

I think I managed to disguise my lack of comprehension. Certainly it wouldn't have done for the native speaker to have been flummoxed by the test. At the same time it was impossible to gauge how the poker-faced students had managed to decipher the indecipherable; the majority of them stared at me as if they were considering what herbs to sprinkle on my slowly roasting carcass. I ploughed on with the second paragraph, adding an unconvincing number of commas, not to mention a full stop which turned into a choke, which in turn evolved into a cough. The final paragraph contained such nonsense that, sympathising with my audience, I very nearly pointed out the translator's failing. However, in a split second I noticed that the entire class was furiously scribbling my every word onto pieces of paper, which seemed to indicate that I must have been making some kind of sense.

Once the ordeal was over I glanced across at Svetlana to get some feedback on my performance, and she nodded her head with what seemed to be approval. My neck, which had been tense throughout the reading, relaxed just in time for me to hear the words, 'One more time please.'

Over a coffee later, I chatted with the students in English whilst Svetlana busied herself marking the papers. The level of conversation suggested just about all of them would be failing the exam. So it was more than a little surprising when an hour later Svetlana returned with a satisfied smile on her face and, having gained the attention of everyone, was able to announce, 'Congratulations – you have all successfully passed the listening comprehension.' I then departed, somewhat bemused by School 777.

I wandered down backstreets, not taking the most direct route back to the hotel. I peered into ramshackle courtyards decorated by washing clinging onto lines that zigzagged across dusty terraces. Houses appeared to have been knocked up with little if any thought to consistency of style: wood met brick which met stones patched up with cloth – chaotic arrangements that somehow managed to be charming, a sign of eccentricity rather than a declaration of poverty. Telegraph poles leant at angles, causing the cables to appear tangled, while weeds offered the drab stonework and cracked, dishevelled paving an illusion of life.

These hidden arteries soon gave way to the streets that ran off from the station; a growing number of cafes and a swanky wine bar with loud pop music pumping inside hinted at proximity to the spine of the city. I found a plastic table and chairs, the one concession to al fresco, outside a small grocer's shop. The only coffee he offered was Maxwell House in a jar, so I took a warm, dusty can of Fanta from the shelf and, seated at the table by the side of the road, amused myself watching life in Ulyanovsk pass me by.

* * *

Departing next morning, I felt sorry to be leaving Ulyanovsk. The city had charmed me. It seemed a shame to have to go. Tram No. 4 deposited me at the bus station, where I bought a ticket for Tolyatti from a pretty attendant with an engaging smile. This is traditionally the realm of the rudest people in Russian public service – put a pane of glass in front of a Russian woman and she turns into Genghis Khan – but even the ticket sellers of Ulyanovsk were charming. In a state of bemusement I climbed into a muddy Renault van, a smile having crept onto my face.

A SMALL ATTEMPT TO REDRESS THE BALANCE OF RUSSIAN HISTORY

It would be unfair, before I leave, not to mention one of the least known of the great Russian novelists. Ivan Goncharov was born in Ulyanovsk, which was then called Simbirsk. As a young man he moved to St Petersburg, where he mixed in literary circles with the likes of Turgenev, Dostoevsky and Grigorovich, a dazzling coterie of minds that collectively became known as the 'Men of the Forties' (the 1840s, that is). Inevitably perhaps, Goncharov took a backseat to his more illustrious companions, despite giving the world Oblomov, a character who personifies the decline of the nineteenth-century landed gentry in Russia.

Oblomov was the second of only three novels that Goncharov was to write. Yet he wasn't idle, and, working as a censor for the St Petersburg censorship committee, oversaw the publication of some important books by the likes of Turgenev, Dostoevsky, Nekrasov and Pisemsky, often meeting with heavy criticism for doing so. When he succeeded in getting Pisemsky's *One Thousand Souls* accepted for publication, he was officially reprimanded by the censors for his troubles, which may have been the spur that he needed. A year later Goncharov quit his job and, in a single month, wrote *Oblomov*, a feat he explains thus:

> *It might seem strange, even impossible that in the course of one month the whole of the novel might be written… but it had been growing in me for several years, so what I had to do now was just sit and write everything down.*

Oblomov was considered in retrospect a Russian classic. Among other achievements, it introduced into the literary lexicon the term *oblomovshchina*, which encapsulates a new type of Russian man. Almost uniquely, oblomovshchina exposes a single but striking feature of Russian society – that of social apathy, a self-destructive laziness, symptoms of which are a complete lack of ambition and an inability to plan beyond the next day. Other great characters of Russian literature had displayed elements of the condition – Onegin, Pechorin and Rudin – but never had it so fully possessed a character as it does Oblomov. The great Anton Chekhov said that Goncharov was 'ten heads above me in talent', while Turgenev said, 'As long as there is just one Russian alive, Oblomov will be remembered!'

CHAPTER FIVE

VOLGA PEOPLE

*'We sometimes encounter people, even perfect strangers,
who begin to interest us at first sight, somehow suddenly,
all at once, before a word has been spoken.'*
Fyodor Dostoevsky

The Renault minibus deposited me and a collection of other travellers at the central bus station of Tolyatti, after our journey just short of five hours from Ulyanovsk. Tolyatti is the mail-order bride capital of western Russia. Over the years many provincial Russian towns have been given this title, but it is Tolyatti that crops up time and time again with this particular label. In this relatively thriving town, men from the West, after months and possibly years of internet-based courtship, arrive to meet the objects of their desires. An interest in cars would be a bonus; Tolyatti is also

140

home to one of Russia's foremost car-manufacturing plants. Possibly the best-known four-wheel creation from Tolyatti in the West is the Lada; taken from the Russian word *ladya*, meaning boat, the Lada is a Russian copy of the Fiat 124.

In 1966 the Soviet government paid the Italian company Fiat one billion US dollars to build the factory which was named after the Italian Communist Palmiro Togliatti. He had died in Yalta two years previously, but not before famously saying, 'Joseph Stalin is a titan of thought. His name is to be given to an entire century.' At the time the factory was the world's biggest. Nowadays Tolyatti continues to be the second biggest car manufacturer on the Volga after Nizhni Novogorod and has been making cars for domestic use and export since the seventies. Interestingly, the cars used to be floated to distribution points along the river until the cost of oil and the privatisation of container shipping pushed the transportation of cars onto the railways.

After a good stretch, a not particularly good cup of coffee and another good stretch, I set off. My plan was to walk the 100 kilometres to Samara, following the course of the river as much as possible over the following few days. I spent the first few hours walking along a dusty path that ran parallel to a busy dual carriageway – heavy trucks lumbered along pot-holed tarmac. It couldn't have been further from my romantic vision of travelling along the Volga:

Lazy orchards and sun-drenched afternoons dozing in the long grass whilst listening to the river wash by. Friendly locals offering hearty meals and banter, perhaps the occasional soak in a steaming hot banya if I was lucky.

It took me half an hour to negotiate a six-exit roundabout, such was the volume of traffic. I saw signs back to the bus station and very nearly gave in to temptation. Yet I didn't concede and by mid-afternoon I had left the town's outskirts behind me. I hadn't joined the river but I instinctively felt that it wasn't far away, hidden beyond the line of trees at the edge of the field I trod through. When I eventually reached the trees and there was no sign of the river, I asked a lady who was digging a hole in the soil, a bag of seeds attached to her waist. She looked at me as if I was mad before furiously shaking her head. My heart sank and my knees buckled as she told me I was some five kilometres from the river and, moreover, that I was heading up river not down.

Before I had a chance to comment, she continued to argue (with herself, presumably, as I was in complete agreement) that there was absolutely no point in travelling the wrong way along a river if indeed there was any point in travelling along it at all. As luck would have it, she clearly took pity on me and kindly offered to drive me back through the town as she lived on the other side and would be going home when she had emptied her seed bag. I sat down and watched her while she finished her work.

The Volga became a valued national resource originally because of its fertility. From the sixteenth century onwards it attracted a mixed and considerable influx of settlers. What had once been a wild province, very much like Siberia, became a familiar home to many. It was on the banks of the river that Russian trade, and in turn life, blossomed. Helped by the persuasive influence of art, over the years the Russians now generally seem to consider the Volga to represent the real Russia, the heart, the salt of the Russian earth. Pushkin, Tolstoy, Nekrasov, Gorky, Bunin, Lenin and others all proclaimed the magic of the river.

Probably the most famous visitor of a creative disposition was the painter Ilya Repin. Up until his visit in the 1870s, the region and the Volga in general had never really been the source of much artistic inspiration – certainly not in the way that Turner had reacted to the natural world. A world-class artist at the centre of the Russian Realist tradition, Repin documented Russians living out their lives in dire social conditions. Ten years after the emancipation of the serfs, he chose as his subject the Burlaki, the last living descendants of the serfs. Repin studied some thirty living characters, filling two albums with sketches, before setting to work on his masterpiece: the prize-winning picture *The Barge Haulers*.

In the early 1800s there were about 600,000 Burlaki, many of them fleeing brutal landowners and their wretched living conditions. One of the very last of their number was the social historian Vladimir Gilyarovsky, who died in 1935. The appeal of the Volga for them was the abundance of food that it afforded them, and the opportunity to forge out new lives.

I shared a seat in my benefactress's car with a hessian sack full to the brim with carrots. As we bounced across the cratered field, those at the top leapt free and scattered, one finding its way onto my companion, who took a bite then discarded the remaining carrot through an open window. She reached for another and did the same thing, then mumbled something about soup and needing some bread, which she emphasised by coughing up some phlegm and launching it through the open window. All the while she punctuated her activity with a vigorous scratching of her head, each time increasing the pressure of her foot upon the accelerator pedal. On arriving back at the road, we hurtled along at considerable speed with many of the dirty orange vegetables now free of their sack. When she reached for a tightly capped thermos, and her intention to pour the contents into a cup became clear to me, I considered whether in the spirit of self-preservation I'd be better off jumping out. Thoughts of ejecting myself were dismissed when the river suddenly engulfed the windscreen, as if the channel on a TV had just been changed. The arrival of the Volga brought much relief and the jeep came screeching to a halt.

Once out from behind the wheel of the jeep the babushka beckoned me towards her small wooden izba, set beautifully only metres back from the river. Once inside, she ushered me to sit on a single metal bed which was the only concession to furnishings in the one-room home. Within moments of my sitting down, the door rattled and a small man with spectacles carrying a leather document case joined us. He did two complete circles, as neat as clockwork, before perching on the end of the bed next to me and introducing himself as Valera. He had returned home, he said, from working as a taxi driver in Tolyatti. He revealed that trade was not so good at the moment and that he was better off in Moscow, but didn't want to leave the old woman, his mother, alone. He went on to tell me that he had returned from living in the USA, where he had driven taxis in Seattle. 'The best place on earth!' he enthused.

Valera's document case was full of different identity cards, which he proudly proceeded to show me. It appeared that at any given time the man with whom I sat on the bed could transform himself into anyone he wanted; he was particularly keen for me to see his private investigator's licence. Valera spoke to me in broken English, very quickly, giving me no time to test his limited listening comprehension, as his mother busied herself over the sink with no small amount of carrots. Our one-sided conversation was repeatedly interrupted by the ringing of his phone, which, when he wasn't speaking into it, he fiddled with in one hand like a smoker with an unlit cigarette. After one such interruption, he said, 'My sister, she works in the presidential office. You want to meet with the president?'

I guessed he was kidding, but the prolonged sincerity of his gaze suggested otherwise and forced a reply: 'Not really.' Even if I'd actually believed this was a meeting Valera was capable of arranging, I could think of no reason to meet Vladimir Putin.

It was then that my companion hit me with his business idea, perhaps hastily put together after having met me, or perhaps always up his sleeve for occasions such as this one.

'Nobody wants to live in Russia,' he said, conspiratorially. 'All Russian people want to leave, and want money. My people are corrupt, the girls they want money, they have sex with foreign man for money.' He paused, closely monitoring my response. 'Now all you have to do is invite Russians to your country and I will put $1,000 into your bank account for each visa issued.'

A bowl of carrot soup was handed to me. Valera's proposal had come as something of a relief. For a moment I'd thought that things were heading in another direction with a more immediate proposition. Unfortunately, however, the relief in my face was taken for something else.

'You like, yes, this is lots of money for you, and very easy. We can start soon, I have girls for you. When, when?'

Valera pushed impatiently like a child wanting to play. But I was feeling distinctly ill at ease. Anxious to escape, I finished the delicious carrot soup, bid my companions farewell and, having first confirmed I was going in the right direction, set off down the river. I had never been very good at business.

***

South of Ulyanovsk the Volga is forced east by the Zhiguli Hills, and follows a big loop before continuing on its course. Give or take a few nautical miles, this is where Valera and his mother's izba was. The Chernetsov brothers, amateur painters who made a Volga pilgrimage in 1838, described the loop as the Samara Bow because it resembles 'the shaft bow that stands upright on a horse's harness'. It was reputed to be the most beautiful part of the river, although nowadays, as many of the liners passed down the river in darkness while travelling at night, it was seen by few. I was interested to see how much beauty actually remained after the Soviet industrial ambitions had taken their toll.

An old willow tree with backcombed branches, standing feet from the water, acted as gate keeper to the stretch I would walk along. As I set off, a large black and white bird glided overhead – it was the first bird I had seen on my journey. I waded through thick, moist grass as a small collective of cows, protective of their lush pastures, looked on. Sporadic bundles of blackberry bushes hung over the water, their undernourished berries like deflated balloons. The water, rust-coloured in places, rippled past carrying occasional flotsam, usually wood of various shapes and sizes; a tyre had been snagged on a protruding rock, so that it appeared to be clambering to safety like a sea lion onto ice, out of the reach of whatever lay beneath the surface.

When I had asked the fisherman back in Kazan what he had been fishing for, he had merely replied, 'Fish'. I interpreted this as meaning, 'Any fish – if, that is, there are any left alive.'

A BANDIT LEGACY

In prehistoric times this whole region would have been underwater. Before the revolution, an aristocrat, Count Orlov-Davylov, ran an estate in the area dealing in timber and sheep. Later, in 1927, the estate became a nature reserve. The trees were mostly lime and oak, with the occasional pine rising up towards the sky.

At the mouth of the bow is the Zhiguli Gate. It is a particularly narrow part of the river, an ideal spot for bandits to sit in wait for their prey. The bands of robbers – Robin Hood-like in their belief they were offering a civic service by robbing from the rich to give to the poor – gave their name to the Karaulny Bugor, 'the lookout rock'. The seventeenth-century bandits demanded levies from the vessels entering the bow, and those who refused were beaten with burning birch branches; perhaps this legacy is what gave the

Zhiguli Hills their name, as in Russian *zheguli* suggests burning. All the greats of Cossack banditry inhabited these hills at one time or another, among these Stenka Razin, Pugachev and Kondraty Bulavin. The latter led the Astrakhan Revolt, or the Bulavin Rebellion as it was also known, which was a war between the Don Cossacks and Imperial Russia in 1707. It has been said that Bulavin was never a particularly accomplished military commander; however, he did have a knack for rallying his people against the Czar, a talent that enabled him to sustain the revolt for at least a year until it eventually petered out. Unfortunately his ability to rouse people didn't stretch to himself, as he was found dead suspected of suicide in 1708.

While the legends of the Zhiguli Hills live on in spirit, the physical habitat has changed immeasurably in the face of massive industrialisation. As the current slowed, I came to patchworks of water lilies. The sun reflected off the pretty pink blossoms, so that for a few moments I persuaded myself that I could see silver scales leaping up from the water. Moments later, rain began to fall, corrupting the smooth, still glittering surface – as I watched, it fell harder and then harder. It was summer rain, and thus warm and refreshing, but it came down with a sting and was no fun to walk in, so I waded through the grass towards a settlement I spotted in the distance, where I would try to find somewhere to stay for the night.

***

Taterov's drab and deserted central square was decorated by several run-down kiosks. These were resolutely closed and, moreover, appeared to have been for several years, with rusted tin roofs and crumbling, cracked façades. The square was fanned by a gentle breeze coming off the nearby hills, which felt pleasant but did little to mitigate the apocalyptic mood of the place. Even less edifying was the sight of a semi-inhabited residential complex, reminiscent of the final scene from *Full Metal Jacket*. Gutted apartment blocks stood grimly alongside others which looked incomplete yet, confusingly, showed signs of inhabitation, not least washing swaying on lines. Clearly the Soviets had left their mark, yet despite their unquenchable thirst for the unsightly, Taterov did still have a beating heart. Well, at least there was one beating heart left in Taterov and that was of an elderly woman selling onions and apples on the edge of the square.

I first came across the phenomenon known as *huzun* on a trip to Istanbul. The word translates as 'melancholy'. However, Orhan Pamuk, Turkey's Nobel Prize-winning author, calls it a comforting type of melancholy; he cites it as the melancholy and sense of inadequacy that has embraced Istanbul since the abrupt demise of the Ottoman Empire, a feeling of sadness that is not private but rather a communal depression – a darkness harboured by an entire city, a condition shared by the whole community.

I had adapted huzun for my own purposes with regards to the Soviet Union: post-Soviet huzun, or as I now called it... *pshuzun* (pronounced with the p and h silent). It was a state of melancholy that could be felt all over the old Union from Tallinn to Vladivostok, a certain depraved sadness that manifested itself in the streets, buildings, people and culture. It was Russia's very own end-of-empire sadness and one that provided nourishment not only for the Russian people but also for visitors: 'How can anyone live in villages like that,' the writer Danil Granin exclaimed as he toured the Novogorod area at the end of the Soviet period. 'Such melancholy.'

The Russian word Granin used for the atmosphere was *toska*, which besides melancholy also contains shades of yearning, nostalgia and even anguish – emotions that suggested these worn and poverty-stricken places were grieving for times past. Typically, only an outsider is able to see the beauty of dilapidation, decay and dereliction – a beauty sometimes accidental yet always a result of time's sculptor chiselling away. For those who live amongst it, as their faces testify, it is no more than squalor, poverty, despair and a constant reminder of the hopelessness of their lives. As Pamuk points out, we who take pleasure in the beauty of such despair – 'historical decay' – are usually from the 'outside'. Pshuzun can only exist if witnessed through the eyes of a visitor, a visitor finding romanticism in what could be someone's everyday miserable life, someone like me... a tourist.

Rich with pshuzun, Taterov was small, with an uneven gravel and dirt track that ran through its centre, lined by tall, sun-bleached apartment blocks in poor repair. Both clothes and people were draped from the overlooking balconies. It soon began to get dark, the solid shape of the sun sinking behind the hills from whence I'd come, leaving orange haloes over the disappearing landscape.

The town, I knew, had one claim to fame: the Georgian writer Alexander Kazbegi spent several months holed up in Taterov due to illness. Kazbegi is best known for his 1883 novel *The Patricide*. It's a story about a bandit called Koba, a defender of the poor against all the injustices thrown up by poverty. Koba had a healthy contempt for authority and a not insignificant belief in vengeance – often violent vengeance. A certain Joseph Stalin, not known for his mild-mannered approach to life, was apparently greatly influenced by both the novel and its protagonist, taking the name Koba as a revolutionary pseudonym for himself. After studying in Moscow, Kazbegi returned to Georgia, where he became a shepherd in order to experience the lives of local people. When he tired of this he became a journalist and later a novelist, seeking to write about the local people he had observed for so long.

The proprietor of the town's only hotel was a very short man, barely five feet high. Taking my passport, he studied my name and declared it to be a Georgian one. And that he should know, he said, being Georgian himself. I didn't dispute this, or his claim to be fluent in seven languages; given the background of the region, this was more than a little bit likely. According to the historian Pliny, the Romans used 134 interpreters in their dealings with the clans of the Caucasus. The Arab historian Al-Azizi called the region the Mountain of Languages, recording that 300 mutually incomprehensible tongues were spoken in Dagestan alone. My host, however, opted to address me in French, to which I gamely responded with my schoolboy vocabulary. My host flattered me that my mastery of the language was excellent. Obviously his own French was elementary.

'Breakfast included,' he offered as a passing shot – or at least I thought that's what he said.

***

Bebur pushed some more of the glittering brown powder into the thin wooden pipe and passed it to the friend who sat beside him. His face was half-illuminated by the flickering candlelight; his dark expressive eyes gazed towards the distant hills. Cheeses of different shapes and sizes were piled on a platter at their feet. The men were smiling and soon Bebur, offering me some more of the heady Moldavian wine, broke into a fit of asinine and highly contagious laughter.

'In my country we don't use glass – it is tradition,' he joked, no doubt to explain or justify the fact that we were drinking from the bottle due to the lack of any suitable drinking vessel. Bebur lectured in technology at a college in Saratov, and his friend Djota was a sculptor from the south of Saratov, a town called Ivanov. There was a third member of the group but he said very little, just sat in his Craig David-style hat and Woody Allen spectacles. At one point he mentioned that he had travelled across Turkey. Otherwise he merely giggled a lot.

The three friends were Georgians. I had met them back at the hotel and they had been fast to invite me to share their bonfire, a short walk away.

'We only smoke at holiday time,' Djota assured me, with a hint of irony on his face, as if keen for me not to get the wrong impression of them. I wanted to believe him, yet there were, I thought, several reasons for doubt, not least of which was the flourishing crop of marijuana on the hills. Also, I wasn't aware of it being holiday time.

Djota's English had been learnt more on the street than in the classroom and his conversation was peppered with colloquialisms. His favourite was 'It's not so important', which he seemed to tag onto most things he said. At that particular time and place, with the sonorous hills and the black and glittering energy of the sky, I was inclined to agree.

'A spa hotel will soon arrive in these hills,' Bebur said with an air of premonition, married to a glint in his eyes. A hotel, package tourists and jacuzzis didn't really sit with the majestic calm of our surrounds. Bebur drew upon his pipe before delivering his verdict: 'A hotel will be very bad I think.' We all laughed; the suggestion seemed so preposterous. He then confirmed, 'No, I think a hotel is a long way off but we see more and more foreign tourists up here.'

Djota added, 'In the name of Iman Shamyl never a spa hotel here!'

'Who was Iman Shamyl?' I asked without thinking.

The faces of Djota and Bebur immediately dropped, while Craig David, having remained still for hours, suddenly jerked to attention. The men's previously benign expressions now turned serious, almost disappointed, as if I'd let them down.

'Yes,' was the only word uttered, falling sluggishly from Djota's lips. The friends then looked at each other as if silently deciding who was going to speak, before saying simultaneously: 'He was a great man.' Moments later Bebur took the baton to speak.

'He was a great warrior and example to all the peoples of the Caucasus.' He paused as if enjoying the feeling of pride he took from even the idea of Shamyl; then he sat upright and, his chest puffed out like a rooster, continued: 'Shamyl was leader of the Muslim tribes of the north Caucasus, most famed for his anti-Russian resistance during the Caucasus War during the nineteenth century. This was the name given to the resistance to the Russian Empire's expansion into the territories of the Ottoman Empire and Persia.' He then took a deep breath and slumped back down.

Some would argue that just as important in the Caucasians' resistance to Russian expansion was a man called Hadji Murad. Leo Tolstoy's posthumously published novel *Hadji Murad* (1912) is a fictionalised account of the man's struggle. Murad was born in a small town called Tselmas. Ethnically an Avar, he was a renowned marksman, famed for never shooting twice at the same target. Curiously, Murad started out on the side of the Russians, but the story goes that he was arrested for a crime he didn't commit and, after escaping from a period of incarceration, became their sworn enemy. He joined up with Iman Shamyl and for many years the two soldiers wreaked havoc on the Russians.

Murad employed many revolutionary tactics, including reversing the shoes of horses to send pursuers in the wrong direction. However, Shamyl and Murad fell out after the former named his son as his successor, a position Murad had hoped for himself. As a result of Murad's angry reaction to this news, Shamyl stripped him of his rank and demanded the war tribute that he had secured earlier in the struggle. Murad replied to Shamyl's request in a letter in which he stated, 'The only thing I have with me is my sword and let Shamyl take it with his own.'

Murad, aware of several plots to kill him, went back over to the Russians' side, taking numerous men with him. Upon learning of this development, Shamyl rounded up and imprisoned Murad's entire family. In response, Murad tried to get the support of the Russians against Shamyl, but they didn't trust him so in turn locked him up. According to Tolstoy's fictional account of Murad's life he was killed whilst trying to escape from the fort in which he was held by the Russians.

Bebur sat back and considered the distant darkness, clearly satisfied with his portrayal of the two great men of Caucasian history. 'Shamyl will never be forgotten,' he concluded. 'Today there is a song people sing to children:'

> *O mountains of Gounib*
> *O soldiers of Shamyl*
> *Shamyl's citadel was full of warriors,*
> *Yet it has fallen, fallen forever...*

***

The following morning I found my way to the hotel bar in search of the complimentary breakfast, the prospect of sizzling sausages and eggs teasing my stomach. Like much of Taterov, the small room with the word 'Bar' scratched on its wooden door was deserted and appeared to have been for some time. I counted four plastic tables and sat down at one. There was no sign of any kitchen, nor any food. As I considered where I would find some breakfast, or at least where I would find a person to direct me to some breakfast,

I was joined by a man. He approached me wielding a metal mug and a tin of tobacco, his Ali Baba trousers flapping, sunglasses crooked on his brow.

'You have hot water for me?' His question was more of a statement, making any attempt at refusal seem both bad manners and a grammatical error. The man perched himself on a chair inches away. His eyes ran me up and down. 'You will not find what you're looking for here. We look for breakfast yesterday… Nada, you have more chance of catching your own. I'm told many boar in mountains. However, if you have a kettle – I can give you Maxwell House.'

He landed a large jar of coffee onto the plastic table. I thought about his strange request and for a few moments thought that perhaps it was quite normal to carry a kettle around. He gave me a look suggesting he knew something I didn't as he presented his hand: 'Bernard from Nuremburg – that's in Germany.' He then proceeded to shake me close to death.

'My friend is resting. He drinks too much, yes, yes, too much!' he sighed, his voice deepening to the pitch of Windsor Davis. His next question actually sounded like a question: 'You want to drink?' He saw my reluctance – it was still morning – so by way of persuasion added, 'It is God's will.' This didn't really convince me as I'd already found out about God's will and alcohol several times in the past.

THE LIFE AND TIMES OF THE VOLGA GERMANS
Germans have quite a history in the Volga region, living on the river around Saratov and to the south.

Recruited as immigrants to Russia in the eighteenth century, they were allowed to retain their culture, language and traditions (not least their churches, which included Lutheran, Reformed, Catholic and the lesser-known Mennonites) by a one-time German princess who became Catherine II. One of her first acts of governance was to invite Europeans to Russia to farm land. English and French colonists were more drawn towards the Americas, but settlers did come from Bavaria, Baden, Hesse and the Rhineland. After the 1917 revolution, the Volga German Autonomous Soviet Socialist Republic (ASSR) was established. Its capital was called Pokrovsk and later Engels.

Then in 1941 the Nazi invasion of the Soviet Union left more than an eye of suspicion glaring at the Volga Germans as potential collaborators. Consequently, Stalin had them transported wholesale to labour camps where many would die of hunger, cold and overwork. By 1942 just about all of the able-bodied German population had been conscripted into the Labour Army or Trudarmii; one third didn't survive the camps. The Volga German ASSR was dissolved and 400,000 Volga Germans were stripped of their houses and lands and transported to Kazakhstan and other isolated regions of the USSR.

The Volga Germans never returned to the region in the numbers that had existed before the war; many remained in the Urals, Siberia and Kazakhstan (1.4 per cent of today's Kazakh population are known to be Germans). In fact, in 1979 there was a proposal for a new German Autonomous Republic within Kazakhstan; but fearing a backlash from Kazakhs and Uyghurs, the Communist Party sacked the idea.

Since the break-up of the Soviet Union, small numbers of Germans have returned to Engels, and today there is a not inconsiderable 600,000-strong ethnic German population in Russia.

Over the next few hours, over a bottle of cognac that Bernard produced from a pocket in his jacket, my new companion held forth on a range of topics.

'These are eccentric boots,' he declared, slapping my feet. 'This is not good for walking.' Bernard then pointed to his own. 'This is very good for traveller; it is very strong,' he said and then, bringing his gaze back to mine, 'this is not good.'

That was sorted out then. I found his childish directness quite disarming. Next was national identity.

'We are human first, second Islam, and third German.' Bernard was very proud and certainly not scared of generalisation.

'England,' he claimed, 'is the only country in the world that doesn't make good cake. Samarkand, España, Germany, they all make great cake!' He fell silent for a moment, allowing his words to soak in, before continuing: 'Germany makes great cake, and yes all, all bad cake in England!' It was difficult to know whether to take him seriously as he spoke deadpan, with no hint of irony.

After some time we were joined by his friend Habba, who had previously been sleeping. Habba, swigging from the bottle, offered me some advice. He had, he claimed, friends in Moscow and should I be stopped or 'hassled' by anyone whilst I was there, I should simply say I was a friend of his. I gazed at Bernard with polite scepticism as he slugged down more brandy.

'Yes, yes,' Habba insisted, 'to any person who wants to stop you at any time, policeman or anyone, just tell them and you'll have no problem. This I think is easy.' It was at that point that it dawned on me that Bernard and his friend were quite bonkers.

'I wish you a good stay in Russia. Tomorrow we find a truck to take us up to the church. You will come with us.'

I was left thinking I had very little choice.

Early the next morning I set out under the control of my German friends, having been assured that this was the best time to head up to Petroshevatsky Sabor, which was the church mentioned by Bernard the previous day. He had also suggested that it was something of a hidden gem, unknown to guide books and many Russians alike. As promised, Bernard had arranged for a pick-up truck complete with a driver wearing army fatigues. This was a local man who touted himself as a guide, although we'll never know if he was equal to his credentials as his English was poor and Bernard did most of the talking.

It was a slow start, courtesy of charmingly obliging local shepherdesses who, on seeing us, would throw themselves into a pose in the road in front of us, displaying varying degrees of exotic coyness in freeze frame until I'd taken several snaps. Such was the enthusiasm of this voluntary modelling corps that it seemed impolite to refuse their advances. None of them asked for money or tried to sell us anything. The fame of being in our albums and memories presumably was reward enough. As each particular shoot came to an end, Bernard would bellow out, 'Bravo! Bravo!' then leap from the back of the truck to bound over and kiss all those involved firmly on the lips – an experience they all seemed to enjoy before running off in fits of laughter. On his return to the truck, standing upright, Bernard instructed the driver at the top of his voice: 'Forward!'

With the distractions out of the way, we proceeded along a narrow road which, occupied by the occasional goat, snaked gently into the foothills through glades of spruce and pine. We passed out of the woods where the road began to level out and hills gave way to the sun-scorched horizon as if melted away by the heat. Our ultimate destination appeared in the distance, and Bernard greeted the vision ahead with the cry, 'Get some of that and then get some more of that! Jeeeesuuuuus!'

I could only agree as my jaw dropped in awe. The church was a truly mesmerising spectacle. Silhouetted by the sun hiding behind its ancient stones, it was a worthy symbol of the region and I found it hardly surprising that, after the shepherd girls of Taterov, it was the second most photographed image in the hills. Bernard and Habba went running off to explore the 'odd girl' (I think he meant 'old') whilst I simply sat hypnotised by the view of the surrounding mountains, enjoying probably the best moment I'd ever had above 5,000 feet.

***

I left the hotel early and found my way to a concrete shelter that constituted the town's bus station. After some not particularly extensive consideration I had shelved my aspirations to walk to Samara... there had been a change of plan. There was a flurry of activity as daylight slowly imposed itself. Minibuses pulled in at speed, breaking hard as if leaving an F1 race circuit for a pit stop; having filled up with passengers, they left just as quickly. I was still sleepy so it was like waking to a world in fast forward. With thirty minutes to wait for a bus to Samara, I bought a coffee from the kiosk cafe and went in search of a quiet retreat to enjoy it. Around the back of the concrete shelter I found a stack of breeze blocks to perch on and settled in to enjoy the strong black coffee and an angular view of the river in the distance. The Volga was now very different to the river of its youth, the river I'd first encountered west of Moscow in amongst the picturesque Valdai Hills. It had grown up increasingly looking like a product of nurture rather than nature. Across an area of sloping wasteland populated with brambles and discarded rubbish, I could make out the solid concrete rim of an aqueduct traversing the barely visible surface of the river. The deep far bank was shrouded by a wall of concrete that hugged the course of the river as far as I could see. The truth became clear, as I sipped coffee from a plastic cup: at this stage of the Volga's journey little remained of the river that had carried me to Tver in *Molly*.

The fifteenth longest river in the world, longer than the St Lawrence and the Orinoco, yet still dwarfed by the three great rivers of Siberia and by the Amazon, Nile and Mississippi, had burgeoned into the product of Stalin's aspirations. Unsurprisingly perhaps, its size has encouraged grand ambitions. The Soviet – or, more specifically, Stalin's – dream was to create the largest working waterway in Europe. Deep enough and long enough to handle a constant flow of freight – barges that would connect the empire from all corners of the globe – it was a superstructure built by an accident of nature.

Nature, however, had made the river slow and often shallow. These were characteristics that didn't fit well with Stalin's vision. Also, the current tended towards the right bank, creating troublesome islands of flotsam, sand and endless marshy shallows.

Even back in Czarist days it had been obvious that only artificial enhancement would make the river useful. And Stalin was determined to make his and an old Russian dream come true. At his command the Soviets dug the Moscow Canal, effectively making Moscow the source of the river, and constructed the seven reservoirs that made her transformation complete. The modern-day Volga is a little shorter than the old one – 1,980 miles from Moscow to Astrakhan. In its Soviet heyday it carried one sixth of all Soviet freight and millions of holidaymakers.

The achievement of what was called the 'Great Volga' was certainly political but the true benefits were economic. The Great Volga linked the heart of the Soviet Union to six of the world's seas. The 80-mile-long Moscow Canal which was Stalin's pet project from 1933 to 1937 involved a 'special Navy' shifting 200 million cubic metres of earth with very basic machinery; the canal linked the capital with the natural river and thus all the way through to the Caspian

Sea. Later the Volga–Don Canal brought the Black Sea, the Sea of Azov and the Mediterranean Sea into the network. The Baltic Canal, which was finished in 1964, opened the way to the Baltic and North seas. The present-day Volga south of Moscow is thus a gargantuan living memorial to a man who himself was a questionable force of nature.

Some, however, would argue that the modern-day, post-Soviet Volga River is the embodiment of all the ugliness of the Soviet machine, an artificial man-made defiance of nature, destructive to the surrounding wildlife and nature. The fish have all but gone, and the fertility of the riverside lands has diminished greatly: Mother Volga's basket is all but empty. Factory chimneys push out constant clouds of smoke; sewage pipes constantly spew pollution into the river.

The Soviet Union has a bad reputation for environmental destruction. However, it is not the only industrialised country with blood on its hands. The Rhine, the Mississippi and the Thames have all fallen victim to the desires of government. Although the tragedy that was the Volga unravelling in front of me was not unique, 'its tragedy is uniquely eloquent', as Gorky once said.

Many, including Gorky, have seen the Volga as a perfect symbol for Russia's continuing and inexplicable self-destruction.

CHAPTER SIX

A VOLGA PARADISE

As I lay on the riverside beach in Samara I watched sapid sunlight slowly settling on the Volga's southern bank. The last few days of travel had left me pleasantly languid, worn by the adrenalin of freedom. A feeling that craves more of the same, that makes one restless and impatient with routine, as well as dissatisfied with comfort. It was probably fortunate, therefore, that I hadn't been overburdened by much of the latter for a while.

Upon arriving on the outskirts of Samara, I had picked up a local bus, still in service some forty years after it had come off the Soviet production line. A short but rocky ride delivered me to Samara's central bus station. From there, on foot, I followed signs to the city centre. It was rush hour in Samara: the pavements were crowded with pedestrians, cars crept along, jammed bumper to bumper; but a simple change of direction, down a gently sloping hill, had brought me to the summertime city, which clung to the river and was quite different to the one bathing in exhaust fumes.

I found a bench to sit on looking out over the river – a scene that staggered my senses, mainly because I'd never seen anything like it in Russia before. The carefree scene I witnessed was more like Long Beach, California, than a conurbation by the Volga River in provincial Russia. The recently surfaced embankment was populated by people furiously pursuing 'leisure'… in an array of formats.

Most striking were the rollerbladers. Some, like Olympic slalom champions, weaved their way at speed through the meandering pedestrians before crowning their display of skill with a flashy pirouette or a sharp halt followed by a short leap backwards. Others, inevitably, were less accomplished, stumbling along flailing their arms in a desperate attempt to stay upright. Cyclists sped by, some upright, others bent over their handlebars, and there were countless joggers defying the hot sun. One man was particularly intrepid, towing, via a harness strapped to his torso, a small cart piled high with bricks.

The beach, which was sandwiched between the embankment and the water, was populated with upright sunbathers standing to attention like army recruits who hadn't had time to get dressed, dotted about the pale sand like small trees rooted down. To me it didn't look a particularly relaxing way of passing the time, although I have been told that, in the interests of an all-over tan, sunbathing vertically is the way to go.

Just as I was taking in this bizarre spectacle my gaze was drawn back to the promenade. Among one of several dog walkers was a middle-aged lady, complete with a golfing visor, who had on the end of her lead a stocky, pug-faced chihuahua-type dog that appeared not to enjoy walking as much as its mistress. The woman dragged her pet along, and then, after stern words with the recalcitrant mutt, began to swing the animal forward, taking its full weight on the lead. I was reminded of a pendulum. I felt like an uninvited guest on the riverside, detached from the rollerbladers, body-beautifuls and cyclists at Samara's summer party. The problem, I sensed, was that I was not a participant; I was a voyeur looking in on other people's lives, with little, if anything, to contribute.

When the Soviet novelist Vasily Aksyonov visited, he was prompted to remark: 'I am not sure where in the West one can find such a long and beautiful embankment.' Yet Samara, which is the most easterly of the Volga towns and sprawls for ten miles along the river, hasn't always been so peaceful. Its twentieth-century history has been tense with conflict. In 1921, during the civil war, the city's Bolshevik forces were led by General Nikolai Kuibyshev fighting alongside the now legendary Frunze and Chapaev. This stretch of the Volga saw some of the fiercest and most pivotal fighting: on winning back Samara, Saratov, Simbirsk and Kazan, the Bolsheviks effectively won the civil war for the future Communist state. As a result, during the years after the civil war Samara and many other places across the union were rebranded in Kuibyshev's honour. It goes without saying that Kuibyshev was murdered by Stalin. Such a respected and honoured man couldn't have been seen as anything but a threat to the increasingly paranoid leader.

Following the Second World War, Samara became a closed city and industrial centre, manufacturing rockets and aircraft, and producing electronic equipment, building materials, clothes and processed food. It has been said that if the entire Soviet Union had stopped working, it would have survived off the back of Samara's production alone.

In earlier days, Samara had been called a Russian Chicago, as it grew very quickly after 1850 with the arrival of the railway, the Trans-Siberian, which crossed the Volga at Samara. Samara was also to be the beginning of the line south to Tashkent and Samarkand. Before the Soviets arrived, it was grain that was important to the city's economy. Along with Ukraine, Samara made Russia the world's biggest grain exporter up until 1913. The region, however, with very hot summers and little rainfall, was prone to famine. The worst of the crisis years were 1874 and 1891 when summer temperatures reached 45°C, resulting in disease, dead livestock and dead children. The Soviets never managed to regain Russia's position as the world's leading grain exporter – collectivisation (Stalin's brutal agricultural policy) brought into play other factors which crippled production.

Samara is also famous as the place to which Shostakovich was evacuated during the Siege of Leningrad – he finished the Seventh Symphony whilst living in the city. Trotsky didn't much care for the place, calling it 'outstandingly philistine, without a university, obsessed with money-making and devoid of all aesthetic concerns'.

By the time I'd taken a wash in the river and lazed away a few hours watching the hobbyists hurtling back and forth along the flower-lined promenade, Cafe Myanoff had come to life. Sleazy-sounding jazz provided a call to arms for lunchtime diners. Deciding to ignore the summons, I left the riverside and soon found myself in a very different city. Revolution Square was worn and overgrown, with battered, uneven paving. Beyond, on Kuibyshev Street, the joyful summer playground gave way to lovely, time-troubled period buildings in pinks and turquoise – faded and jaded, but all the better for it. I walked over to the futuristic train station which, helpfully, displayed Latin translations. WaytoRussia. com said of the station: 'the Samara train station is a real surprise', and they are not wrong. Among other things it is one of the tallest railway buildings in Europe, at 93 metres, with a 14-metre spire and an open observation deck 64 metres up.

Completed in 2008, Samara Station seemed somehow out of step with the multitude of Russians milling about in its pristine surrounds. Here the crowds appeared more suited to the imperial degradation of the stations I knew in Russia, not Saturn 9. There was nowhere, it seemed, to put the bag ladies, the waifs and strays; it was these that gave the character and colour to the stations I'd frequented in the earlier stages of my journey. The station was functional, clean and sleek, but it was no fun, despite an upbeat song that was playing – 'Samara Samara Samara' – suggesting it should be fun.

Unfortunately, the receptionist at the Transit Hotel was not quite so forward-thinking as her surroundings suggested, refusing me a bed on the grounds that I had the incorrect registration. I was directed up to the service centre, where I was told I would be able to sleep in a chair. Despite the fact that I had been looking forward to sleeping in a bed, I felt surprisingly unfazed by the prospect. I'd done it before, with satisfactory results, and I'd do it again.

The service centre operative was a warm and friendly girl in her twenties, who gave the impression she wanted to redress the balance after my experience in the Transit Hotel. Before I could say 'mine's a recliner' she had placed a cup of tea in front of me and allotted me a very comfortable-looking leather chair. How long would I like? Six hours would do nicely – it cost two hundred roubles, which at the time was less than five English pounds and, I considered, quite the bargain. The Transit Hotel could stick their comfortable beds and hot showers. I'd stay here to the crack of dawn and then head to the river for a swim. Everything had come together nicely, I thought.

I finished the tea and closed my eyes, my head resting on the cool black leather. Then, for the first time, I noticed a five-note electronic burst that was sounded like a fanfare before any announcement was made. It sounded just like that used in seventies stylised mysteries at key turning points in the plot. For the next hour, slumped in the chair, I actually thought I was now part of such a TV show, until eventually I drifted off into the world of sleep. Once there (although my memory is vague), I spent the next few hours as Dick Barton's special assistant.

***

One of the delights of the city's riverbank was the view across the Zhiguli Hills. I had spent the sunset of the previous evening watching the boats from the ferry port loading up with vehicles, their destination the spectral beaches and homesteads visible across the water. The famed outlaw Stenka Razin had hidden out in the hills during his heyday of anti-Czarist activity. This area, specifically known as the Samaskaya Luka, was my planned destination for the next few days.

I'd been in contact with Samara Tours. They were very keen to include me in a small group rafting trip that would be departing from the ferry port at midday. I was excited about the prospect, not least as I saw it as an opportunity to be guided – a welcome chance, in other words, to rest my own decision-making muscles. I was looking forward to being able to sit back and look around, enjoying the luxury of somebody else worrying about the details. Just like all the tourists back in Sergiev Posad, I could relinquish all responsibility for a while.

Samara Tours had offices on Kuibyshev Street, just along from Revolution Square. Steep, uneven steps ascended to a mustard-coloured townhouse equipped with a heavy wooden door. Anna was to be our guide and tour manager. She was a pretty girl who, from the first glance, offered reassurance that she would be able to handle a few rapids with a bunch of tourists. She gave off an aura of calm and confidence, and I liked her immediately. She proffered me a seat in a cold metallic office – and I was quickly with a cup of coffee.

She turned to her computer and began printing pages out. After a small pamphlet's worth of paper had flunked onto the table below the printer, she stapled them together and handed them to me.

'These are some of the excursions we will do – please look. We will be joined by three others who I believe would enjoy better the level one so if you have no problem I think we will do the level one.'

I flicked through the 'brochure'. A cursory look revealed over ten levels and well over ten possible excursions, at least twenty different variants. Anna had obviously given me the information as a tease, however, and she had made it very clear that we would, in fact, only be doing one. I thought back to the menu at Hotel Venets in Ulyanovsk with the six different pasta dishes on offer when it was only ever going to be pasta with fish. Even if I'd turned up at Samara Tours decked out looking like a champion rafter I was only ever going to be offered level one with fish. As I certainly wasn't a champion rafter I was able to confirm to Anna that level one suited me just fine.

Fittingly, we set off in a Zhiguli jeep with the raft attached to the roof. I was sharing the expedition with Katya and Alex, a couple from Moscow. Both had default expressions that gave the impression they had far more important things going on elsewhere. Otherwise, the most striking thing about the couple was that Katya had a good foot in height on Alex. From behind especially, when holding hands they resembled a mother and son, so that on those occasions when they entered into activity of a more romantic nature it was somewhat alarming. The other member of our collective was a Norwegian scientist called Florence, a wiry lady with unflattering round spectacles over which she peered before talking. In contrast to the others, she wore a look of constant concern.

Anna seemed perfectly unfazed by her group. Indeed, her voice seemed to take on wings as she gave us some background on what we would be doing, when we would be doing it, and who had done it before us, as well as no small amount of information about the legend that was Stenka Razin.

Razin first appeared in history in 1661 as part of a diplomatic mission from the Don Cossacks to the Kalmyks. The same year he went on a pilgrimage to the Solovetsky Monastery on the White Sea, for the 'benefit of his soul', after which all trace of him was lost. Six years later he reappeared as the formidable leader of a band of robbers based at Panshinskoye, in the marshes between the rivers Tishina and Ilovlya, from where he was able to acquire tribute from vessels passing down the Volga. As the 1654–67 war with Poland put pressure on the Russian people, Razin's marauding ranks began to swell with men who travelled south to avoid conscription and heavy taxes.

Stenka Razin's life and deeds make a great story, and one that Anna told with relish. I had known that there was more to the man than simply having had his name borrowed for a brand of Russian beer. Razin's original aim, to loot villages, is not contested; however, he also became a symbol of the peasant unrest of the time as his movement turned political. The Cossacks, of which Razin was one, supported the Czar and autocracy, but they wanted a Czar who would respond to the needs of the people, not just the upper classes. Razin believed that by plundering towns and villages he was able to redistribute power, giving more autonomy to the peasants.

The rebellion didn't end with his death in 1671. The rebels of Astrakhan held out for another year before the Czar restored control. Razin's movement had failed, and as a result there was increased government control; it was a reaction that has been seen time and time again throughout Russian history. That said, as historian Paul Avrich put it: 'Razin's revolt awakened, however dimly, the social consciousness of the poor, gave them a new sense of power, and made the upper class tremble for their lives and possessions.'

RAZIN'S LEGACY IN RUSSIAN CULTURE

Razin is the subject of a poem by Alexander Glazunov, a cantata by Shostakovich and a novel entitled *I Have Come to Give You Freedom* by Vasily Shukshin. He is also the hero of a popular Russian folk song written by Dmitri Sadovnikov. This song in turn provided the title for a well-known Soviet musical comedy, *Volga Volga*, the melody of which was used by the Seekers in a song which made number one in Australia and the UK in 1965. The lyrics of the song were dramatised in one of the very first Russian narrative films, *Stenka Razin*, directed by Vladimir Romashkov in 1908. The film lasts a brief ten minutes and the first verses go a bit like this:

> *From beyond the wooded island*
> *To the river wide and free*
> *Proudly sailed the arrow breasted*
> *Ships of Cossack yeomanry.*

On the first is Stenka Razin
With his princess by his side
Drunken holds in marriage revels
With his beauteous young bride

From behind there comes a murmur
'He has left his sword to woo;
One short night and Stenka Razin
Has become a woman too.'

The queue onto the ferry was nine cars back, but Anna reassured us there would be space on the ferry and boarding would only take half an hour. After an hour and still no gangplank, Alex began to pace, furthering my suspicion that he had matters of a more urgent nature to attend to. I felt like telling him that there was nothing more important now for 48 hours and, besides, we were in Russia. This, of course, he was more than aware of, which perhaps is why he was pacing.

Once the jeep had been jammed onto the crowded ferry, Alex's apparent impatience abated little. I'm sure at one stage I saw him looking at his watch and tutting. Consequently I feared for how relaxing this trip was going to be. Florence, on the other hand, was taking the delay as an opportunity to have a snooze. Anna was able to hide any frustrations she might have been harbouring with her enthusiasm – reassuring the group that we would only be on the ferry for 20 minutes. I myself was happy to spend all night on the ferry. Having been on my own journey for several weeks now, I had sunk into a world where time had taken on a comfortable degree of insignificance, and I was grateful to be in the company of other people.

And because I'd entered such a state of abandonment, I felt privileged just to be squeezed into my half-seat on the Zhiguli. I wanted to know my companions, whatever misgivings first impressions had offered. The uncomfortable ferry across the Volga that late afternoon was a spiritual joy, full of hope for what lay in wait. The sun was setting as I watched the riverbank rollerbladers shrink into the night while the peninsula to which we were heading took on a reality beyond the romance I'd created over the past two days from the Samara shoreline.

The ferry came to an abrupt halt, which brought Florence to attention, looking around with a glazed 'who the hell are you?' look. Alex and Katya started jabbering in fast Russian clearly designed not to be understood by us – yet clearly understood by tone as further moaning. Base camp proved to be a tried-and-tested patch of ground with a bell tent and scorched earth, a few hundred metres back from the ferry drop-off. We were in the Zhigulis, a range of wooded mountains which are an important source of oil. The particular part of the mountains we would be calling home was set within a pretty copse of birch and beech trees, the ground covered with patches of bluebells and buttercups.

* * *

Anna was quick to distribute tasks. Alex and Katya, still jabbering away in indecipherable Russian, were asked if they wanted to continue their conversation whilst preparing the food for dinner. Much to my surprise Katya was quick to simply say 'No!' Alex reassured Anna that he would be happy to and, as he said this, rolled his sleeves up. Meanwhile, Florence volunteered herself as fire-maker, and I helped Anna erect a tarpaulin. Camp was soon made, a fire was roaring and Alex proved himself very capable in the kitchen, serving up a chicken-and-rice dish equal to anything I'd eaten on my journey so far.

Inside the bell tent there was room for six hospital-style metal beds. I had a choice of two, the others already having been bagged. When we eventually turned in for the night, after Anna had advised us that we had 'a long day ahead of us', I discovered I was next to Florence, who under the illumination of a head-torch proceeded to unpack her backpack and arrange the contents with the precision of a surgeon preparing her theatre. This went on for some time, accompanied by various mumblings. When she was fully satisfied that everything was neatly in place she undressed with equal attention to detail, illuminated by the light from her forehead.

My head found its way under my pillow, where thoughts of Florence were replaced by the sound of Alex and Katya still talking to each other at speed. I drifted off to sleep only to be awoken some time later by the sound of a foghorn. Florence, it transpired, was a snorer and the sounds emanating from her direction were those not of a human being but rather of a not insignificant ship. Her camp bed vibrated with the force of her exertions. I passed a sleepless night.

Next morning, Anna and I carried the raft about fifty metres to the river. On a map, the Samarskaya Luka looks like the head of a turkey; its semi-oval shape lends itself to raft racing perfectly and therefore it is no coincidence that its reputation as a circuit is legendary. Every year hundreds of locals raft *Zhigulyovskaya Kruglocvetka* or 'Around the World', as it's known, although nobody seemed to know why. I wasn't sure that any of us were up to rafting around the world, but we would get a great insight into the national park and all that it had to offer.

With the raft bobbing on the clear, gently rippling water we were joined by Florence. She was decked out like a triathlete in a wetsuit straight out of the packaging, the black rubber shimmering in the rising sun, whilst an oversized water-sports helmet made her quite unrecognisable; in addition, a water bottle hung from her long neck and she even had a whistle strapped to her wrist. Alex and Katya followed close behind, their attire suggesting they were somewhat more relaxed about the day on the water. Alex, in fact, was very much more relaxed, apparently about everything – perhaps having talked through all his concerns during the night.

He was the first to climb aboard the raft and took his position at the helm in a clear statement of intent. I had met Captain Pasha back in Volgaverkhovye – was it, I wondered, now the turn of Captain Alex? He would certainly have a lot to live up to. However, having seen Alex installing himself, Anna shouted with some force, 'Move to the top side please, whilst people are embarking.' Anna's command made perfect sense as Alex had already caused a not inconsiderable imbalance to the vessel by seating himself at the stern.

Katya was next on, proceeding like an anxious tightrope walker over eggshells. Florence and then I followed. Then, with all aboard, Anna cast off and the current slowly pulled us away from the shore.

Anna steered with a light touch, occasionally dipping her short paddle into the clear water to make the slightest alteration to our course. Most of her labours went unnoticed – she made it look so easy. The raft lightly skimmed the surface of the water, gaining pace as we got further away from the bank, making the sound of a leather whip gently cracking against wood. We continued this way for two hours or so until Anna gestured towards a small beach where we stopped for lunch. Along with lettuce-and-tomato rolls, Anna fed us much information about the picturesque national park we now found ourselves in.

The Samarskaya Luka, or Samara Onion peninsula, consists of 32,000 hectares of national forest reserve which has earned the nickname of the Russian Switzerland – a frequently used nickname for several regions of Russia that retain much of their natural beauty. Anna, despite her apparent love for the peninsula, was realistic with regards to its undeserving nickname.

'Of course, it does not hold the beauty of Switzerland, but some of the most beautiful views of the Volga can be seen here.'

The time we spent on the beach was punctuated by requests by Alex to take the paddle for the next part of the trip. Anna eventually gave in to his demands but first she told us about the Grushinsky Festival, probably Samara's best-known event, taking place in July every year. It had its genesis in the 1960s when 'Author's Song', a form of musical poetry, gained popularity among intellectuals; it is a type of folk music that is difficult for foreigners to appreciate. Every year musicians gather in the Zhiguli Hills National Park to perform their songs, as many as 100,000 people arriving from all over Russia and the CIS. The festival was named after Valery Grushin, who was a member of the trio Singing Beavers. He died in the sixties whilst saving children from drowning in the Uda River in Siberia.

Sitting at the back of the raft, paddle to hand, Alex was like the cat who had got the cream. The growth of the smile on his face seemed to correspond with the growing amount of foam and white water we skimmed across. More and more rocks popped up as obstacles, and increasingly I hoped Alex would relinquish control back to Anna. However, when asked by Anna, 'Would you like a rest now?' Alex's response was, 'Don't worry, I'm fine – you're in safe hands.'

Soon afterwards we hit a particularly rough section of the river, which caused the bow to snap at the waves and rear high into the air, water spraying back over us in the raft. My heart leapt as for a split second the bow was nearly vertical; the girls screamed and clung to the rope that ran around the perimeter of the boat. Moments later we became horizontal again and I looked back to see how our temporary skipper was doing, only to find that he had vanished.

With stomach-sinking surprise, I realised that Alex had gone overboard.

A grim silence set in as everybody realised what had happened. I soon caught sight of him flailing around beside the raft, his head intermittently disappearing beneath the surface of the water. Katya was the first to speak when she revealed, somewhat matter-of-factly, 'He's not a very strong swimmer.' Under the circumstances this was not encouraging news.

By the time I had actually registered the situation, Anna was reaching out over the side and soon had a firm grip on Alex's hand. It was pretty simple to go over the side of a raft; but getting back in was another story. Alex wrestled with the raft's solid ridge as we continued along the river, completely out of control, before he flopped out of the water like a seal, collapsing in a deflated and very wet bundle in the reassuring embrace of Katya.

Florence remained unmoved by the whole episode, whilst Anna calmly resumed her position at the back of the boat, bringing a cool air of control to proceedings. Unsurprisingly perhaps, we didn't hear much from Alex for the rest of the excursion. He spent much of the time clinging onto Katya with a concerned look on his face.

The trip had taken us 30 kilometres from base camp so that night was to be spent at an 'authentic' homestead in the hills. After a short climb along a rocky pass we were greeted by a wooden board with the words 'Stenka Razin was here' carved onto it. Seeing this, I was a little sceptical about the dwelling's authenticity. A jet ski parked up on a trailer in the yard to the fore of the concrete bungalow added to my scepticism. A man in a tatty suit with a heavy chain hanging from his neck and a bulky watch on his wrist appeared and started enthusiastically chatting with Anna. It transpired that the homestead was Samara Tours' 'official' homestead and that Gregori, the besuited man, was our host for the evening. Gregori waited for us all to gather before addressing the group. I had been bang on with my assessment.

'Welcome to the Zhiguli Hills, my friends; you will have much pleasure here tonight. My name is Gregori, and I am the only living relative of the great man Stenka Razin.'

A look of disbelief descended on the faces of everyone present. The only exception was Anna, who simply nodded as if saying, 'Oh yes, we've really saved the best for last, haven't we?'

Gregori could have told us anything – that he was Peter the Great's cousin, Lenin's great-grandson or Yeltsin's brother – and I probably wouldn't have doubted it. But a relative of Stenka Razin living in the Zhiguli Hills – nah! That was just too convenient. Alex and Katya looked on at Gregori with expressions of sympathy. Florence simply wasn't having any of it.

'Can I please see my bed now?' she barked, adding 'Mr Razin' at the end.

After my initial surprise at the extent of the subterfuge, I warmed to Mr Razin, and saw the opportunity for what it was. How many people can claim to have spent the night with a blood relative of possibly the most famous Russian outlaw? Not only was he a potentially huge name-drop, Gregori proved to be an accomplished cook; nor was that the full extent of his talents. The first part of the evening was spent relaxing in the banya, Gregori having heated it earlier in preparation. After eight hours of rafting down the river I could think of nothing better – sentiments shared by Alex and Katya. Apparently Florence could and did think of something better and, having found her bed, remained there for several hours. Or at least so we thought.

Once we had sweated out the day's exertions and returned to the bungalow, it became clear that sleep hadn't been Florence's only distraction. Under the close guidance of Gregori Razin, we found her busying herself in the kitchen. As the evening unfolded, it became undeniably clear that despite her initial annoyance she had taken quite a shine to the fifteenth-generation descendant of the notorious bandit king, often to be seen gazing at him and listening intently to his every word.

Anna, having passed all responsibility to Gregori, spent most of the evening on her laptop. Gregori, however, proved a congenial and generous host. Once we were fed and watered he led us out to a fire pit overlooking the river. The lights from Samara on the opposite bank illuminated the night, and the occasional craft crawling home. Once blackcurrant chai and vodka had been generously distributed, our celebrity host settled himself amongst us, and proceeded to sing. Was there no end to his talent?

Gregori Razin sang beautifully, although his set was a little limited; I heard the mention of Stenka Razin in each song several times. Whether he had bandit blood running through his veins or not, Gregori was a delightful man. Once he had called it a night, after many requests for an encore, a toast was suggested. So we all filled our plastic mugs and brought them together with a clunk over the fire, whilst Gregori proposed the only toast he could have done at that particular place and point in time: 'To Stenka Razin.'

The following morning Anna assembled the group early; she appeared refreshed and vital, more than could be said about the collective she now surveyed, whose edge had certainly been filed off the previous night. A ride by jeep took us back to base camp, covering the ground much more quickly than the previous day, and from base camp we travelled back across the river by ferry. The tour had been too short; helped by our evening with Gregori, we were now beginning to feel comfortable with each other – no mean feat as we had come together as quite different people just 48 hours earlier. On reaching the agency back in Samara, we all bid our farewells and I watched my fellow rafters drifting off into the late morning. I followed Anna back inside the building, as my business with Samara Tours wasn't over yet. I wanted to go on a very different type of tour, one that would take me underground, and Anna knew the perfect guide.

***

Riding in a battered taxi, my new guide Shevadze halted the driver outside an austere building on a leafy street. We had stopped outside the Office of the Public Defender. My guide cleared his throat and stared at me with his icy blue eyes.

'So, my friend, which Georgian do you think of before any other?'

If I'm honest it was Katie Melua who came to mind. But I wasn't given the chance to test Shevadze's sense of humour.

'Stalin!' he interrupted. 'You and the whole world think of Stalin.'

Despite Katie's ever-growing profile and the fact that she has sold well over a million copies of her first album, he was probably right.

Stalin somehow still felt like a dirty word – the unspoken, something not altogether accepted. Britain has Churchill, Shakespeare and Dickens, while America has Elvis Presley and Abraham Lincoln – entertainers and, arguably, people who have changed the world for the better. Georgia has a mass murderer responsible for the deaths of millions – not necessarily something to celebrate.

'Yes, Stalin is the most famous Georgian,' he said. 'However, a close second has to be Beria – you know of Beria?'

I confirmed that I did. During the 1930s he was the Communist Party kingpin in the Caucasus and Stalin's most feared henchman.

'This was his home in Samara for a time.' Shevadze pointed over to the current Office of the Public Defender. The irony didn't pass me by, as I imagined the terror that people would have derived from this now apparently nondescript local government building.

'However, I haven't brought you here to show you a boring old municipal office, although I do like this neighbourhood. No, I've brought you here to show you history, history that very few visitors get to see in our city. Beria was not a relaxed man.' Something of an understatement I thought. 'He worried about his protection. He suffered what do you say, paranoia? So he built a series of secret tunnels under the city. They begin here at his house and stretch several blocks through the city. You want to see?'

Beria was born near Sukhumi in Abkhazia in 1899. His mother was a deeply religious woman and spent a considerable amount of time in church – in fact she actually died whilst in church. Beria joined the Bolsheviks in 1917.

He began his career in state security at the age of 20 in 1919, working in the Azerbaijan Democratic Republic.

A couple of years later he joined the Cheka – the original Bolshevik secret police and the template for today's FSB in the Russian Federation. In 1921 Beria was very much involved in the Red Army's invasion of Georgia and the subsequent formation of the Georgian SSR. In 1926 he was made head of the Georgian OGPU, the reincarnation of the Cheka, and it was at this time he was introduced by Sergo Ordzhonikidze to his fellow Georgian Joseph Stalin.

Beria became a strong ally in Stalin's rise to power, but some argue that he was always operating for himself and saw his relationship with Stalin as a way of penetrating the highest echelons of the Soviet regime. He was appointed Secretary of the Communist Party of Georgia in 1931. In 1934 he became a member of its Central Committee. It was at this point that Beria started turning on members of the Communist Party. In 1937 he said in a speech:

> *Let our enemies know that anyone who attempts to raise a hand against the will of our people, against the will of the party of Lenin and Stalin, will be mercilessly crushed and destroyed.*

The Great Purge in which he played a significant role was as severe in Samara as anywhere in the USSR, and included fellow communists and intellectuals. Not only politicians were rounded up and executed, but also non-political working people. Stalin made Beria deputy head of the NKVD

(The People's Commissariat for Internal Affairs) in 1938, which oversaw the police and security forces. Throughout the Soviet Union the Great Purge saw the execution of millions of alleged 'enemies of the people'; it got so bad that the oppression started damaging the infrastructure and the economy of the USSR, which forced Stalin to slow it down. Even the NKVD was purged – Beria surrounded himself with loyalists, usually from the Caucasus.

In 1940 Beria sent word to Stalin that the Polish prisoners of war being kept in camps in Belarus and Ukraine were enemies of the people. As a result, all 22,000 were executed at the infamous Katyn Massacre. Once the Germans had been pushed from Soviet soil, it was Beria's job to deal with those accused of collaboration among the many ethnic minorities: Chechens, Ingush and Volga Germans were all deported to Soviet Central Asia.

Things went downhill for Beria after Stalin's death; however, he maintained positions of power until his arrest in 1953 when he was dismissed by Khrushchev. He went to trial and was found guilty of treason, terrorism and counter-revolutionary activity. He was sentenced to death. According to one account, when the death penalty was read out, Beria fell to his knees begging for mercy, wailing hysterically. In 2003 the archives from his case were released and it was revealed that Stalin had been collecting evidence against Beria for years. Not least incriminating were several claims of sexual assault against him. Many women succumbed to his advances in exchange for the promise of relatives being freed from the Gulag. In an interview in 1990 his wife Nino said of these allegations of sexual predation, 'Lavrentia was busy working day and night. When did he have time for love with this legion of women?'

Although state and former secret police archives contain no mention of the tunnels in Samara that Beria is said to have built for the security of the Soviet elite, the story persists, and it soon became clear that my guide Shevadze was very much in on it. Once I'd asked the taxi driver to wait, Shevadze led me around the back of the block to a garden courtyard. In the corner was a stone bunker or industrial-strength garden shed. Fiddling with a key in a padlock, Shevadze unlocked the steel door and led the way through, descending some steps. At the bottom, approximately ten feet beneath the ground, was an unassuming cement passage with Soviet-era floor tiles visible beneath the dirt underfoot.

Shevadze produced a torch and lit the way. The tunnel itself was visually pretty dull; however, an offshoot from the tunnel's main artery proved extremely interesting. A thick round door opened into a corridor lined with heavy metal bars studded with knobs. Halfway along this passage was evidence of another door, now rusted and broken. The passage, which was about 19 feet long, came to an abrupt end at a cement wall. Shevadze stopped and looked at me with an expression of childish excitement.

'So what was the reason for the tunnels?' I asked, unsure. Samara was never going to be at threat from an attack from above.

'I think for Beria's safety, perhaps. Although I think it is more likely for Beria's romantic life. Or rather, his unromantic life.'

It is believed that Beria was personally involved in executions, rapes and other torture during his career. I got the picture and it sent a shiver down my spine. Shevadze had brought me underground to show me the place where Beria tortured and executed both his own personal enemies and 'enemies of the people'.

My guide appeared to gain satisfaction from my discomfort. He placed the torch on the ground and squatted down with his back against the dirty wall.

'This place is good for you to see,' he said. 'I think it helps explain Russia. Ours is a complicated country. We are a product – as is everyone – of our history. The past is our present, which is in turn our future.'

As he spoke, Shevadze's features were hidden by the dark, but I knew his gaze was fixed upon me.

'However, in Russia,' he continued, 'we choose to ignore our past, as does the rest of the CIS. I am an honest man; I know who I am. I am not a good man, there are many bad men in Russia, but what can I do? We have what we have and must live with this.'

I was disarmed by Shevadze's words. Ten feet underground in a dank and eerie bunker haunted by ghosts from a not so distant past, Shevadze wasn't forcing anything upon me, simply offering me an opportunity to formulate my own ideas, and it was certainly a potent breeding ground. After sitting in silence for several minutes, he cleared his throat and spoke.

'Somebody from the council stumbled across the tunnels when working on the water drainage system. I've never been beyond this door.' He shone the light on the rusty door. 'However, if the tunnel does continue it will have to cross a very large tunnel that is used to carry excess water from underground streams to the Volga River. Eight such tunnels dating back to the Czarist era criss-cross the historic neighbourhoods of Samara.'

As we both sat in the tunnel, any fears or concerns I might have entertained about Shevadze dissipated. On the contrary, I felt an increasing warmth towards him, and was able to share his considerable, if somewhat confused, love for his city and his home.

'There is talk that others have found similar tunnels around the city, but it's only talk – they are, what do you say, mythology. The Institute of Marxist–Leninism in the city is now being demolished and the construction workers have said that a tunnel can be reached from the fountain in the building's courtyard. But I have seen no facts to prove this. However, there are other tunnels that have been verified. There is one in the hillside of the botanical gardens that dates back to Czarist times. During Soviet times the tunnel was used as a secret laboratory.'

Shevadze pulled himself upright, suggesting it was time to leave, before something else caught his thoughts.

'It hasn't been possible to confirm tunnels under Parliament and under the old Ministry of Internal Affairs, although it has been said that Gorbachev used the Parliament tunnel in 1991 when he was president to escape from armed opponents.' Shevadze took a deep breath and then led the way back to the surface and out into a bright sunny day.

Shevadze had suggested, and other historians have concurred, that it is no coincidence that scholars are choosing not to take the opportunity to gain knowledge and understanding about their own history and that of the Stalinist period. Perhaps there is simply some human behaviour that can never be understood. The man himself, however, laboured under no illusions and was, in fact, quite at ease with his own DNA. 'I know who I am' echoed in my ears as we emerged into the garden, all the more colourful after the gloom of the tunnel.

CHAPTER SEVEN

TATTOOS AND TRAINS

I slid the door open to compartment nine on the 5 a.m. train to Volgograd. My cabin mate sprang up from her bed and in one extended movement switched the light on.

'I wasn't asleep,' croaked the diminutive woman in late middle age.

The initial meeting with a cabin mate on a Russian train is often an odd experience. You come together as complete strangers, compelled to share a cramped and therefore intimate space for hours and, possibly, days on end. It's important, therefore, to put your companion at ease as soon as possible, especially if you are, as I was now, the new arrival. I was anxious to get some sleep but for the sake of ingratiating myself with Tina, who appeared to be travelling alone, I was prepared to delay putting my head down.

Yet before I could say, 'Good morning, you just get back to sleep', Tina was making tea. This, I knew from experience, wasn't a good sign: the making of tea meant many things and, funnily enough, sleep wasn't one of them. As a matter of fact, Tina's sudden animation suggested to me that she had been lying on her bunk, biding her time in the empty compartment, waiting for the train to pull in at Samara and for me to clumsily clamber into the cabin.

Tina, I learned, was on her way to her sister's dacha from Moscow, where she had left her husband. Her sister had taken the same train but, because of financial constraints, was travelling in the third-class open carriage. I had done this before, between Moscow and St Petersburg, and a fine and memorable experience it had been, albeit one that had precluded sleep. Tina, I noticed, didn't seem to be struggling with the relatively luxurious surrounds in which she found herself whilst her sister roughed it out further down the train. However, it soon became apparent that she was in the midst of some sibling dispute which was being played out, as so many dramas are these days, by text. After several messages had pinged furiously back and forth, however, she did reveal, somewhat reluctantly, that her sister would be joining us for breakfast. Upon hearing this, the part of me that was looking forward to a good sleep immediately sank.

After going underground with Shevadze I had spent a few more days in Samara. As suggested by Polina, the summer atmosphere was pleasant and a good place to spend a relaxing few days lounging on the riverside beach. To this end I had gone in search of a longer-term sleeping solution than a chair.

I had happened across Hotel Pio, an 'Italian'-style guesthouse, whilst searching through hotel bookers online. I had immediately been seduced by photos of a cute little guesthouse, recently restored according to Italian interior design, and the repeated use of the word 'homely'. It looked great, and even better for having rooms with balconies that looked out in the direction of the river in the distance. I made the reservation – paying the full amount up front.

On arriving at the guesthouse I had been quick to divine that I was indeed the victim of some fairly handy photography. Hotel Pio was Italian in nothing but name. Svetlana's guesthouse was in fact two bog-standard Soviet-style apartments joined together. A wall had been knocked through, various renovations had been made to accommodate the above, and the result was a five-bedroom Italian-style hotel… Soviet style. However, the décor soon became irrelevant, by virtue of Svetlana having two very young babies. The night had passed to a soundtrack of the two babies discovering that the louder they screamed and cried, indeed the more attention they would get. I had been looking forward to the train to Volgograd, if for no other reason than to catch up on some sleep.

***

Russian Railways operates over 86,000 kilometres of track, which makes it the second-largest network in the world after that of the United States. It is also one of the largest companies in the world, employing some 950,000 people.

Its predecessor, Soviet Railways, ended operations in 1991 with the collapse of the Soviet Union. In January 1992 the Ministry of Russian Railways was founded and subsequently the railways entered a period of steep decline due to lack of funds and a dearth of substantial investment.

In 1992 freight traffic fell by some 60 per cent because of the decline. This greatly affected the Russian economy since the railways were the only reliable transport system in the country. In a land of low automobile use, poor roads and vast distances, trains were of vital social importance to low-income citizens in particular, who made heavy use of them. Modernisation, therefore, was vital.

In 1996 the government started to look into the rebuilding and development of the network, examining systems around the rest of the world, and also the Soviet system and the imperial system before that. The programme they came up with was put into motion in 2001, and in 2003 Russian Railways was created as a public company, separating it from government control. By 2005 passenger traffic was up some 30 per cent and the reforms appeared to be working. It was recently announced that Russian Railways was hoping to buy a large stake in PSA Peugeot Citroën, the main distributor of Vauxhall and Opel in Europe.

Over our first cup of tea Tina told me about her great sadness. Stuck within the claustrophobic confines of the compartment, I had no choice but to listen. I knew all Russians carried a great sadness (outwardly manifesting itself as pshuzun) but Tina's sadness, it soon occurred to me, was possibly a little greater than average.

Her daughter lived far away in Canada, having joined the fifth wave of emigration and married a Canadian research scientist. As a result of this relocation Tina's granddaughter, now aged five, was growing up speaking English. Tina's attempts to learn the language had so far been unsuccessful, which meant that, as her granddaughter spoke no Russian, she and the little girl were unable to communicate. Moreover, Tina got very few opportunities to visit Canada, and her daughter seldom came back to Russia. Her frustration was compounded by the fact that the other grandmother was always there, ever present, constantly able to etch her personality onto the child.

I could imagine the scenario: an unknown foreign woman turning up every couple of years from a faraway land, speaking a strange foreign language alien to the little girl. Accordingly I sympathised with Tina – given the time of the day, probably a little less than she would have liked, but my feelings were genuine just the same. The scenario was no doubt common among Russians of a certain generation whose children had become adults during the nineties and looked beyond their own chaotic, futureless country for stability and hope, leaving behind parents in the autumn of their lives on the other side of the world. I had already met men who had been left behind back on the road to Nizhni Novgorod; I was now staring at a mother who had been similarly discarded.

Conversation was a little one-sided with Tina. I didn't mind, happy to simply listen and nod at the right moments or change the expression on my face accordingly. Oddly enough, the one piece of information she was keen to extract from me was how long it took to fly to Scotland. I wasn't able to offer an exact figure but she kept returning to the subject. I was convinced that, based on what she was telling me about her family in Canada, she had perhaps got Scotland confused with Nova Scotia.

Some hours later the atmosphere became more tepid as Tina's stocky sister, who clearly had slept very little (for possibly several weeks), arrived in our compartment. Tina started to empty the contents of a bag onto the small table: tomatoes, cucumber, rye bread and even a small amount of chicken. She insisted that I partake. Unusually for me, I had boarded the train prepared, having loaded up with a collection of 'just add hot water'-type meals in plastic containers. But there was no room for refusal, so I got stuck in under the rather hostile gaze of the sister.

Soon daylight appeared beyond the grubby reinforced window, offering a distraction. Rough, uncultivated land zipped past for miles, muddy brown, punctuated by fields of withering sunflowers and stony ground. A couple of hours after breakfast the train slowed and pulled into a small town some 50 kilometres short of Saratov, at which point Tina gathered her belongings and bid me farewell. I watched her join her sister on the platform and cross over the tracks before vanishing into the austere Soviet station building.

I took the opportunity of an empty compartment to touch base with Vicky:

Me: Just left beautiful Samara heading for Saratov b there soon!
V: Gr8! Hurry up... I will never get married again lol!
Me: Hope not... can't get any more time off.

With the passing of time, love had blossomed and at the same time the problem of the distance between them had increased. Vicky was still living in the UK whilst Dmitry was now building his empire with increased vigour in Russia. However, Dmitry had a solution to this problem of their long-distance romance – a solution he would disclose if Vicky joined him in the country of his birth, Ukraine, for a couple of weeks in September.

Lichtenburg Station in East Berlin is where Vicky caught the 9.40 train for Kiev. The platform on which she had stood for some thirty minutes in readiness for the 23-hour trip was now dark and cold, populated by luggage-laden travellers. However, she was invigorated, her long dormant spirit of adventure awakened. As the train pulled away from the station she felt, for the first time in a long time, at one with herself. Certain about the direction she was heading in. She spent the journey reading the poems of Anna Akhmatova (who had been born in Ukraine) and Taras Shevchenko and staring out of the window at the desolate and bleak Polish and then in turn Ukrainian countryside. The latter poet had a profound influence on Vicky, as she was deeply touched by a man who like no other reached into the Ukrainian soul. So touched was she that on reaching Kiev she missed the daily train to Odessa by nine minutes; a similar situation at home and she'd probably have not missed it, but such was the reliability of the eastern European train network that the train had pulled away from platform twelve at eight o'clock on the dot. The bald-headed guard, with huge upper legs and a fire-breathing dragon tattoo clinging to the back of his neck, had finished waving his fluorescent green baton around just in time to concentrate all his energy on a look of sympathy, as she panted the last few steps to the realisation she wasn't going anywhere that day. She wasn't all that bothered.

Stepping off the train onto the platform at the classically grand station in Odessa, which had been built in the second half of the nineteenth century, she was gripped by excitement fused with a little trepidation. She knew very little about the place other than its infamy for girl trafficking and its 142-metre-long Potemkin stairs – made famous by Sergei Eisenstein's 1925 film *Battleship Potemkin*.

Battleship Potemkin is about the 1905 mutiny by the ship's crew against the officers of the Czarist regime. At the Brussels World Fair in 1958 it was named the 'greatest film of all time'. The film's most celebrated scene is the massacre of civilians on the Odessa steps (Potemkin stairs). The Czar's Cossacks march down the steps firing volleys into the crowd. One victim is a mother pushing her baby in a carriage – as she falls she pushes it away – the carriage rolls down the steps amongst the frantic crowd. The massacre never actually took place; however, the American film critic Roger Ebert says this:

That there was, in fact, no czarist massacre on the Odessa steps scarcely diminishes the power of the scene... It is ironic that Eisenstein did it so well that today, the bloodshed on the Odessa steps is often referred to as if it really happened.

Reference to this scene is also made in a Crunchy Nut cornflakes commercial – and it was thoughts of that which caused Vicky to chuckle as she dismounted the train.

But it was neither girl trafficking nor the film (nor an ad for Crunchy Nut cornflakes) that had provoked a severe case of the jitters. No, it was an overwhelming realisation; she would claim it had taken hold on the train from Berlin, but as she and I both knew, it had been there since leaving the Hermitage all those months ago in St Petersburg on my Imperial Gems tour. It was a realisation that, whatever path her life would now take, it was out of her control and she had very little choice. Whatever the options presented to her, she would be following her heart – along whichever train track that led her to Dmitry. Whether she liked it or not, she was now a visionary with the belief that the heart should be ignored at her peril. She was now a romantic and fully involved in the fight that pitches the logical and clinically-thought-through process of reason against the forces of chaos that ultimately give us what we need… including a little happiness.

It was during their time together in Odessa that autumn that Dmitry (oh so traditional Dmitry) had proposed to Vicky, without a bowl of cornflakes in sight, on the Odessa steps. She had enjoyed that moment, so confident by then of her response, able to allow herself time to be distracted by a mother rescuing her young child from a screeching tumble down the iconic steps, and then feeling she had even more time for her response. In a slow, drawn-out conclusion of the inevitable, she simply replied: 'Go on then.' This took a few moments to digest, but once Dmitry had grasped the situation he quickly followed her positive response with the suggestion that she move to Russia so they could be together. Vicky hadn't faltered and they were soon making more plans into the night. Six months later they were sharing an apartment in Astrakhan, the home of Dmitry's most recent project.

***

Tina's departure left me feeling empty. Such is the contradiction of a train compartment; when she was with me it had been too small for the both of us, but now that she was gone I wanted her back. Rail travel, much like all travel, has a way of accelerating the development of connections and producing bonds which, in my experience, seem somehow fraudulent: real only for the time you are together and so easily abandoned and forgotten. Time spent going somewhere with complete strangers in a confined space provides a potent mix. I felt I knew Tina quite well, yet I didn't know her at all; as when viewing a photograph, I had created all the extras, all the questionable subtext in my own head – my imagination had created what I believed I knew of Tina. The truth was she had simply moaned a lot for several hours. The gap left by Tina wasn't empty for long.

***

This particular length of track ran parallel to the Volga and occasionally I was able to catch a tantalising glimpse of blue passing in the distance. More visible were the concrete blocks, adorned with numbers, spaced at regular intervals by the side of the track. These unnecessary carbuncles displayed the distance in kilometres from Moscow and, unlike many of the rusting and time-ravaged signs that flew past the window, were in a condition that suggested they were cared for on a daily basis. I could only assume their sole purpose was to induce sleep for the weary train traveller. Occasionally we would rattle through villages, logs piled high outside bland izbas.

Next down the aisle were the business-like Sasha and Sergei. They confidently made their entry into the compartment and, with an air of the habitual, made themselves at home in a very short space of time. Tina was quickly forgotten as, lying on my bunk having given up on sleeping, I watched the two men order themselves with the care and precision of those living on a small boat. Once settled, their gaze fell on me and the necessary task of sussing their travelling companion out began.

They were company men on a business trip for the Russian arm of BP. Oil was their line and they were proud of it. They were on their way down to Baku in Azerbaijan. (I was never sure why the oil company with all its wealth didn't see it as advantageous to fly the two men, rather than have them languish on a train for four days out and then four days back to St Petersburg... but I didn't like to ask.)

Sergei was the older of the two men by a couple of decades. With a worn look of resignation on his face, he lay back and read for most of the ride. Sasha was more animated and keen to stamp his status on the new dynamic in which he found himself. He was quick to tell me he was ex-special forces, and to illustrate his point – literally – he removed his T-shirt to show me the artwork on his back. A set of inky wings spanned from shoulder blade to shoulder blade. His face filled with pride.

Tattoos are a popular way to show your membership of a group. In Russia they are especially popular with criminals, and Russian criminal tattoos have a complex system of symbols which give detailed information about the wearer. The area of the body on which they are placed is meaningful too; for example, the initiation tattoo of a new gang member is usually placed on the chest and may incorporate a rose (a rose on the chest is also used with the Russian Mafia). Wearing a false tattoo is punishable in the criminal underworld, and tattoos can be removed by bandaging magnesium powder onto the surface of the skin, which dissolves the skin with painful caustic burns.

Tattoos made in a Russian prison often have a distinctive bluish hue to them as ink from a ballpoint pen will have been used, and they appear somewhat blurred because of the lack of instruments in prison for drawing fine lines. Sometimes the ink is created from burning the heel of a shoe and then mixing the soot with urine, then injected into the skin using a sharpened guitar string attached to an electric shaver. I know all this because I once spent 36 hours on a train from Tomsk to Irkutsk. I shared my compartment with a young man returning home after spending three years in prison for armed robbery. Dmitry had been a wealth of information about many things, not least the artwork that decorated much of his own body, most of which he had done himself. He seemed to be completely reformed and planned to open his own tattoo parlour in Irkutsk.

Tattoos may also be used to stigmatise and punish people within the criminal community, for failing to pay a debt or breaking the criminal code in some way. Tattoos on the forehead are usually forcibly applied to humiliate the wearer and to warn others about him (or her). They can indicate the wearer is a member of an offensive political group or has been convicted of a crime that is disapproved of by the other prisoners, such as child rape. The Russian criminologist Yuri Dubyagin has claimed that during the Soviet period there existed 'secret orders' that any anti-government tattoo should be 'destroyed surgically' – and that this procedure was usually fatal.

The writer and tattooist Nicolai Lilin, author of *Siberian Education*, is one of the leading authorities on this subject. Born in 1980 in the small republic of Transnistria, Nicolai gained his education whilst a member of the criminal gang called the Siberian Urkas. His upbringing was defined by a complex set of rituals and strict codes of honour, in which crime was a constant. His community harboured a deep mistrust of outsiders, especially the police and state authorities, and even the youngest of their children were taught to use violence. By the age of six, Nicolai's uncle had given him his first knife, and by the age of twelve he had been convicted of attempted murder. His book offers an uncomfortable insight into the murky world that exists behind the tattoos.

Lilin says in his book that the oldest tattooing community is that of Siberia, where the criminals created the tradition of tattooing in a coded, secret manner. This was then copied by criminals in prisons all over Russia, altering the essential meanings of the tattoos and how they were translated.

Here on my train to Volgograd, Sasha's tattoo branded him as part of the questionable (in Russia) community of good guys – the police.

I immediately liked Sasha; his particular brand of self-confidence had a way of rubbing off. Perhaps it was simply because I knew that I would be safe with him around – he was a man who, after all, could probably kill with his bare hands. He had critical but gentle eyes. As the fields rolled past like a video on fast forward, magazines were passed round, word puzzles played: a painting by Picasso, five letters? Sasha showed film clips on his phone of the heady days when he arrested gun traffickers – kicking them close to death. Which had what I think was the desired effect of shocking me.

Around midday we pulled into a station at Greezi, a small insignificant backwater. It was lunchtime, and the platform spilled over with kiosks and vendors selling snacks and refreshments. Sasha insisted on locking the compartment, not prepared to take any chances with opportunist thieves. Everyone from the carriage vacated, including a heavyweight circus man and his family of feral-looking children and two performing dogs.

When we pulled into Saratov it was night, and with the deftness of cat burglars my two companions collected their belongings together. As with Tina before them, they departed without sentiment, quickly vanishing beyond the platform into the dark. The 30-minute stop gave me enough time to stock up on Nescafe sachets and potato pancakes.

Saratov started life in the sixteenth century as one of several fortresses (others included Samara and Tsaritsyn or, nowadays, Volgograd) intended to protect the Volga River boundaries from marauding bandits. All three forts were located in a region where the Volga and the Don flow nearest one another. The supplies for building the town were shipped along the river, allowing Saratov to be constructed in just a few short weeks. In a couple of centuries it had grown into an important shipping port. Saratov was a closed city until the end of the Soviet Union, because there was an important military aircraft manufacturing plant in the city.

With 30 minutes to play with, I wasn't going to see a lot, but what I did see wasn't pretty. On the other side of the station building I found myself part of a small crowd watching two young men kicking and punching the stuffing out of one another, blood spraying from both their faces. Quite unnerved, I quickly moved on, trying to appear as purposeful as I could. It was as if Sasha and his video had been the warm-up act. My purpose led me straight back to the platform, which in turn led me straight back to my compartment and bunk, where I realised the romantic Russia of my imagination had itself just taken another kicking.

However, all was not lost for Saratov as they had a particularly successful bandy team, high flyers in the universal bandy league. My *provodnik* (assistant in the train wagon) took it upon herself to explain the game.

BANDY UNDER THE MICROSCOPE

Bandy is played on a pitch the size of a football pitch and follows very similar rules: two halves of 45 minutes, two teams of 11 players, and a round ball.

Some fourteen countries participate in the annual Bandy World Championships, but the only three countries to have ever won are Finland, Sweden and Russia – perhaps performance on the bandy pitch has a direct relationship to national vodka consumption.

The train pulled away with me sitting alone in my compartment, excitement preventing me from even thinking about going to sleep. After a while the door slid open. Silhouetted against the light from the corridor, a smartly dressed bald man in a tweed jacket stood surveying the scene. The man ignored his bunk and instead began to unpack the contents of his bag onto the table by the window: food, vodka and a dog-eared novel. Then, showing no interest in me, he proceeded to take off his clothes and hang them neatly on the hanger at the base of the bunks before lying down on the bed and pouring himself a glass of vodka. I watched, fascinated, as, propped up on his elbow, he knocked the vodka back, closed his eyes and appeared to drift off to sleep.

After several hours I awoke to find him munching on something whilst reading his book. I then took a trip down the corridor to the WC, which revealed that all the other compartments were now empty, leaving me and my new companion and the replacement *provodniki* the only occupants of the carriage.

A ghostly atmosphere had descended. It was quite a departure from the bustle of the first part of the journey, reminding me of what it used to feel like being still at school after everyone else has left for the end of term. After a few hours, my companion became more animated as the small space in which we sat filled with vodka fumes. Watching him, it took me a while to decide who he reminded me of, but then it hit me: he was a weather-beaten Homer Simpson, a vodka-swilling, chain-smoking cartoon. When Alexi, as he introduced himself, discovered that my destination was his home town of Volgograd he got very excited, drawing map after map – each sketch becoming more embellished as the vodka went down.

'I have a very bad cold, but the vodka helps,' he assured me.

Later the *provodniki* talked me into buying a lottery ticket. I sceptically handed over 100 roubles, not entirely sure how I could ever claim my winnings if, indeed, I happened to win a prize. Under the cover of darkness we chugged through the outskirts of Volgograd and approached the central station. Encouraged by a now very enthusiastic Alexi, the *provodniki* switched the carriage's lights off so that we might better appreciate the illuminated memorial to the Battle of Stalingrad, now that the daylight had been replaced by night beyond the train.

Silence descended as we passed by a gargantuan statue of Mother Russia, a majestic and colossal figure lit up not 50 metres away. Shortly afterwards we arrived at the station, where we walked beneath a huge mural on the high ceiling that depicted Stalin amongst a cluster of spiralling images. In addition, portraits of Stalin glared from at least two of the walls.

Alexi insisted on taking me up to the Mamaev Kurgan, this being the memorial complex, of which the statue I'd seen from the train was the biggest star. This is the main memorial to the Battle of Stalingrad and I was grateful for the offer, saving me time not having to find the right trolleybus. Russian war memorials are, by nature, significantly larger than life, but nothing could have prepared me for this goliath of a spectacle. Groups of people, predominantly young couples, appeared out of the darkness to make their way down the steep steps to the road into town.

The long tree-lined avenue leading to the main body of the memorial helped build a feeling of anticipation. The many couples were clearly using the setting for dates which were in varying stages of progression. Love born from brutal war, I concluded, could only be a good thing.

The numbers involved in the Battle of Stalingrad are too big to comprehend: 600,000 Russian dead and an equal number of Germans deceased. In November 1942 the German 6th Army launched an attack on Stalingrad city centre, which was defended by the Soviet 62nd Army. After four months of some of the bloodiest close-quarter fighting seen during World War Two, the Russians eventually came out as victors of a battle that was to have a huge impact on the overall outcome of the war.

The memorial complex was commissioned after the war and built between 1959 and 1967. Vasily Chuikov, who led the Soviet forces, is buried there, as is the famed sniper Vasily Zaytsev. During the Battle of Stalingrad, Zaytsev is reported to have killed 225 enemy soldiers, including 11 German snipers. After the war he settled in Kiev, working in the textile industry, and he died there in 1991, just ten days before the final curtain fell on the Soviet Union. His dying wish was to be buried at Mamaev Kurgan.

There was a crisp chill in the air, which suited the atmosphere. The 83 metres of Mother Russia bore down on present-day Volgograd, sword aloft, her fierce expression more than a little intimidating. A memorial to the dead, it both recalls all that was preserved and acts as a potent reminder of the negligent role of governments the world over and in Russia in particular. In May 2009 it was reported that rising water levels had caused Mother Russia's foundations to subside and that a lean of some 20 centimetres could well cause the statue to collapse.

Alexi bought us both a beer from the kiosk at the tram stop. For quite some time he had said very little, merely passing on facts and figures like a tour guide, as well as filling me in on a few life-affirming anecdotes involving the famed sniper Zaytsev. However, the facts and figures were cushions, buffers, protection of sorts against the harsh and brutal reality of what had taken place on the site of Mamaev Kurgan. Once all the information had been proffered and then digested, you were left with nothing, just an empty feeling: empty because death leaves you with nothing, leaves you empty. By stealth a dirty feeling enshrouds you – not something you can simply scrub off as the dirt is flowing in your blood.

***

Alexi lived with his wife Nataly in a two-room apartment on the third floor of a block opposite the austere Lenin Square. Of all the towns and cities I'd visited, this one alone still shouted Soviet Union from the rooftops. Most emphatic was the Stalinist central train station with its socialist realism murals painted on the ceiling and, every now and again, a picture of Stalin's face appearing in cameo. To me, Volgograd felt strong, special because of its past, in a strange way sacred; yet at the same time it was dated, an anachronism, one BIG museum.

I felt relaxed under the careful guidance of Alexi and yet at the same time restricted; his offer to stay with him had been gratefully received, but I had felt there was little choice, such was his insistence. I always got a buzz from arriving somewhere new and finding my own way. Thus, grateful as I was for the friendship, the truth was that he was cramping my style. At the same time, despite ostensibly feeling free, I sensed some unspoken, unseen control from a higher force, a fear of not doing the right thing or, worse, doing the wrong thing. Maybe these thoughts were emphasised by the constant reminders of the Soviet legacy.

Alexi introduced me to Nataly, his wife of twenty years. She was a handsome lady who wore a persistent expression of intrigue on her face. Her short bob with an abrupt kink at the bottom certainly imbued in her an old-fashioned appearance. The pair of them had obviously missed each other the two weeks that Alexi had been away, on business in Irkutsk, and consequently I couldn't help thinking that my presence was an annoyance, although they appeared perfectly happy to share their love for one another with a stranger. They were, it appeared, proud of their affection for one another and I quickly felt at home. Nataly made us tea and began rustling through cupboards for plates and snacks, but Alexi dismissed the idea of tea and instead produced three bottles of beer.

Alexi's apartment could only be described as dishevelled, but I found it all the more endearing and homely for it: a large single room, high ceiling, with open doorways off to a kitchen and bedroom. Stripped floorboards complemented wallpaper from another decade. A bookcase with a dusty glass frontage, apparently ubiquitous in Soviet-era interiors, dominated whilst a table set for a meal filled the space. Photographs in gaudy frames decorated every available flat surface. As I took it in, it occurred to me that the interior was no different in style to those of apartments I visited in Leningrad some twenty years earlier. I felt like I was stepping back in time, the rugs and the cabinets packed with porcelain items that would never be used. Nataly was an English teacher and tour guide, which went some way to explaining her pleasure at having netted a bona fide 'English tongue specialist', and she was quick to expound the delights of their home town from a tourist's point of view. I hadn't really considered Volgograd as much more than a stopover but, listening to my hostess, I realised that there was a good week or two of exploration to be done.

Funnily enough, at no point did either Nataly or Alexi talk about my trip as if I was free to decide. Indeed, I had the feeling that by passing over their threshold my journey had become theirs. Whilst being very grateful for the wealth of information I was receiving, I couldn't help but feel a little protective of my journey and, more to the point, the control over it that I felt I had lost. My generous hosts were quickly becoming the personification of Russia itself, with its ability to overwhelm and to dominate in so many ways.

Possibly of more concern, there didn't as yet appear to be anything conditional about their kindness. Alexi and his wife didn't seem to want anything from me, merely my company. Why did this feel so compromising? It occurred to me that the generosity of others is almost easier to take if some kind of contract has been entered into, an agreement laying down the ground rules, from the start. I was unsettled by my own inability to accept the positive sides of human nature. The divan was pulled out in the sitting room for me to sleep on.

The following day I was invited to visit Nataly's community centre, which was used as a school for children with learning difficulties. When she had used the term I thought of table-tennis tables, pool tables and Subbuteo football. These images were soon forgotten. The 'centre' was effectively a seventh-floor studio apartment, a big open space littered with a few chairs and equipped with a kitchen area separated by a counter. Through a set of sliding doors there was a balcony with a wonderful bird's-eye view of the city. Yet perhaps the most spectacular sight was the statue of Mother Russia on the other side of the river. It rose in the distance, illuminated by a sun now at its zenith.

Nataly made us all coffee and I glanced around the centre, where teenagers were engaged in various activities, some drawing, others reading. All the equipment in the apartment had been begged, borrowed or stolen. Alexi was one of the centre's scroungers and had become quite adept at acquiring 'stuff'. The coffee machine that now gurgled and spat as if waking from a hundred years of underwater sleeping had been found in a dustbin.

'Simply thrown away – with a little tinkering and it's working again,' Alexi enthused, although Nataly wasn't so enthusiastic.

'Yeah, straight out of the eighties,' she joked. 'I wouldn't get your hopes up. For some reason the coffee an "Ufessa 70" churns out never gets particularly hot, as if programmed at the wrong temperature. Perhaps coffee was drunk cooler in the eighties.'

The three of us laughed in collective doubt that anything could have been cooler in the eighties.

'The sofas – now they weren't so easy to get up here.' Alexi had caught me scanning the space inquisitively. There were three altogether, all tatty and worn, but still in working order; in fact, as we stood by the counter, all three were being utilised.

Alexi continued and a smile appeared on Nataly's face to suggest she knew the story.

'The first one,' he said, pointing to a mustard yellow three-seater, 'well, that was simply too big to fit in the stairwell so we cut it in half and then banged it back together in here, although you can hardly tell.' He looked over at his work with pride.

'We learnt our lesson so decided with the other two, and indeed with any subsequent large items, to hoist them up the side of the building. So we pushed out the balcony windows and dragged them up the wall using a rope. The second one,' he added as, with the same amount of pride, he pointed to the blue sofa, 'came up no problem. However the third one, which is roughly the same size and therefore should be about the same weight, didn't.'

Alexi shook off a look of bewilderment and smiled. 'It was that much heavier, in fact a lot heavier, so that me and the two guys pulling from up here just couldn't work it out, and of course we couldn't really see the sofa clearly. We had to stop eventually – our faces were red with exhaustion. Then when I went down to see what was going on from the ground I could see this one, this one and this one, clinging for dear life onto the inside of the sofa.' He pointed to three kids who were on the other side of the apartment, painting onto a large piece of paper.

'They had attached themselves to the sofa, and now found themselves dangling outside the fourth-floor window, fifty metres above the ground.' Both Nataly and Alexi were looking over at the three with the warmth and pride of parents who wouldn't tell them but in fact were quite pleased that they had been naughty.

Nataly then added, 'How they didn't fall and kill themselves, I don't know.'

This provoked a look from Alexi that could have been interpreted as 'What a very English thing to say. They didn't fall because they are Russians.'

Meanwhile, Nataly wanted to tell me about the genesis of the school. This began in 2008 when Mrs Ban Soon-taek, the wife of the UN Secretary General Ban Ki-moon, visited School 142, a Moscow institution that was at the forefront of a UNICEF-supported programme to include children with special needs in the classroom – a show of patronage which encouraged the project to grow. Nataly had been working at 142 at the time and, thoroughly inspired, had decided to try and duplicate the initiative in Volgograd.

'For decades disabled children – and adults of course – were practically isolated from society, which had almost no awareness of people with disabilities. They were ignored as monsters.' She paused to reflect, then continued: 'Until only very recently, children in Russia with special needs had only two options, either to study at home or be enrolled in a specialised "correction" school. Now UNICEF are working with organisations in Russia to promote tolerance within society. This is only a start in Volgograd, but resources are very small.'

Introductions began with an ungainly boy called Andrei. He must have been about 15 and looked particularly uncomfortable in his skin. His eyes were wide and blue and nervous, but he politely shook my hand and asked me if I wanted to play chess with him.

Then there was Galya 1: the first of three Galyas I was to meet at the project that day and indeed the tallest, by quite some margin. In fact she was the tallest kid in the project altogether. Nataly put it down to radiation, while Alexi attributed it to her family having moved from Tbilisi to Volgograd, where the climate and the milk are conducive to big bones. An open and smiley face made her a warm and attractive girl.

Galya 2 was, by contrast, the smallest kid in the project, coming in at just over five feet, and also probably the roundest. Galya 3, meanwhile, was timid and shy, mumbling a greeting through a scarf that came up over her chin.

Another girl, Tamara, also caught my eye. She was elegant and graceful and, at 14, carried herself with the confidence of a much older girl. Her English was as solid as her confidence and she fast emerged as the most competent within the group, so that I often called upon her to explain or translate.

The trio surfing the sofa were named Ravi, Giorgi and Sara. Ravi and Sara were brother and sister, born only hours apart. Giorgi was the group comedian, always ready with a quip and a joke. I could tell, by the tender fashion with which Nataly passed on these extra details about the kids, that she was really fond of them. I left thinking that I would very much like to return sometime. The work Nataly did with the able assistance of her husband was admirable; what she was able to give to 'her' children was precious indeed. It was only a shame she was able to help so few and had to work so very hard just to give them the time and support she did. Despite my initial resistance to Alexi's kindness, it had now dawned on me that he wasn't being 'Soviet' in his hospitality but simply human. He and his wife truly were like a couple of Samaritans; without Nataly and the centre I couldn't help but think what would become of the children I'd met. The warmth and spirit injected into my own journey in Volgograd, in stark contrast to its history, spurred me on in good spirits towards my now imminent reunion with Vicky and the subsequent wedding, but not before one last gesture of kindness from Alexi.

***

After my experience on the good ship *Sable* I would have been quite happy to take the train for the final leg down to Astrakhan. However, in my heart of hearts I knew that the only way to arrive at the wedding and to conclude my journey was by boat. I needed to actually be on the waters of the Volga River, which had been my companion for the past two months. This was a belief shared by Alexi, who told me – leaving very little room for discussion – that he would be taking me down to the ferry terminal and putting me on a boat. As luck would have it, he knew a man, who knew a man who could help.

Alexi's friend ran his enterprise from a small rented office in a building just round the corner from the central station. To reach it we had to pass through a shambolic shopping arcade jammed with concessions selling everything from electrical goods to women's clothing, and then negotiate a corridor piled high with brown sagging boxes which spilled loose papers expelled by the weight of those on top. Wires ran along the floors and walls as extension cord linked to extension cord, and there were piles of old browning newspapers covered in dust. A plastic Christmas tree balanced on a stand in a corner as if patiently waiting for the festive season.

Upon seeing us, a warm-smiling lady beckoned us into her room and pointed to a couple of chairs. Alexi explained my situation and the woman spat out her reply so rapidly that I could only pick up the odd word. Alexi summarised things for me when the lady had fallen silent: in short, there was a ship leaving that very afternoon aboard which I could ride all the way to Astrakhan, and the journey would take about 40 hours. If I wanted it, he continued, there would be no charge other than a $200 administration fee.

Alexi's expression told me that he thought this to be a very good deal. I wasn't so sure; I could only believe that for that price there would be luxury involved in my accommodation beyond my needs. However, I put up no resistance. I was grateful to Alexi for his help and a little bit of luxury never hurt anyone. I was fast to surrender my mind to thoughts of a palatial cabin with panoramic views across the river, and the finer things I'd yet to experience – en suite with a king-size bed, dinner at the captain's table followed by ballroom dancing...

CHAPTER EIGHT

A VOLGA FUNERAL

*'Nature creates whilst destroying, and doesn't care whether
it creates or destroys as long as life isn't extinguished, as
long as death doesn't lose its rights.'*
Ivan Turgenev

The MS *Lermontov* was 60 feet long, low in the water, and similar to many boats I'd considered with delight from the safety of the shore during my journey. The wooden gangplank wobbled on the heavy chains by which it was suspended as I boarded, to be greeted by Igor, who shook my hand before leading me to my quarters. The main accommodation block, I noted as we descended through the bowels of the ship, was below the bridge and well below water level. It contained a neat Formica-finished galley with a stove and a basin, similar to that found in a small campervan, as well as a seating area with two leather sofas positioned at right angles and a small TV set.

A doorway led to Igor's cabin. There was a brass plate on the door with the word 'Captain' engraved upon it. My cabin lay forward towards the bow and came equipped with a sofa on which to sleep and sit, plus a washing machine and freezer, both of which Igor told me were used by the crew. Contemplating the arrangement, it didn't take me long to conclude that my cabin was, in fact, the ship's utility/laundry room. No matter. It might not have been the royal suite of my imagination but I was grateful that it smelt of fresh washing rather than dirty smalls.

During my guided tour I was introduced to Vasily, the ship's engineer, and Petrov, the ship's cook. Vasily was carrying a few extra pounds and wore an easy smile that made me feel welcome. Petrov, by contrast, was unhealthily thin and carried an anxious expression that made me want to get him to a hospital. The rest of the crew was made up by the first mate, a man called Ron from Armenia, and by Alexander, who hailed originally from Moldova. Alexander seemed not to have a specific role; instead he sat around a lot and, on more than one occasion, I came across him lying on my sofa.

In fairness to Alexander, he was a cold-weather specialist and bad-weather navigation was his thing. Consequently his skills were mostly required during the winter months; during the summer period most of the navigation could easily be done by those on the bridge. He also didn't get paid very much.

I joined Igor and Ron up on the bridge as we pulled away from the port. Unfortunately, this distinguished position didn't fill me with confidence, appearing to be something of a dumping ground for unwanted bits and bobs. Bundles of rope, broken winches and defunct radio sets made their home amongst other examples of now equally useless seafaring paraphernalia. The display of junk made me think of Pasha from Volgaverkhovye who, I'm sure, would have speedily put it up for sale on eBay.

Fortunately, Igor seemed at ease amongst the debris of past voyages, which helped to soothe my own concerns. As we set out among a flotilla of smaller craft, he told me about his varied cargo: office furniture flat-packs – for the Gazprom offices amongst others down in Astrakhan – were stowed alongside thousands of packets of 3-in-1 Nescafe coffee and boxes of washing-up liquid. Ensconced in a swivel chair behind a panel with radar and satellite navigation screens, a small tiller to hand, Igor looked every bit the captain and, thank god, seemed very relaxed.

Soon a nameless town slipped by on the eastern shore, its golden-domed and abruptly square Orthodox church dominating a cluster of ramshackle izbas, all of them with neat vegetable plots. I took myself along to the bow to escape the noise of the engine. This vibrated through the heart of the vessel with the rhythmic beat of the piston. The boat was working hard, and well it might be: it was over half a century old, having been built in the then Czechoslovakia in 1955. As I sat on the bow with my legs dangling over the side, the first drops of rain came down, gentle summer rain initially, which gradually got harder and eventually graduated to a full-blown thunderstorm which I opted to enjoy from the bridge.

Towards evening time the skies cleared and the sun appeared from behind the clouds to reveal – well, nothing much in particular. Russia was unrolling on either side but the banks of the Volga were so far apart at this point in the river that it was impossible to make out much detail other than low-slung flatlands splattered with occasional trees, the odd horse and rider and a fisherman nestled into the grassy banks here and there.

Eventually, the dull riverscape was interrupted as the first significant town made its appearance. The golden onion dome of its Orthodox church gave it away, reaching up above a small peninsula we were rounding. As the *Lermontov* groaned around the jutting embankment, more and more of the town was teasingly revealed, like nervous children poking their heads out from behind a doorway.

Attractive two-storey houses lined the bank of the river. Some boasted window boxes overflowing with colourful flowers; others turned to the world scarred with cracked panes of glass. A goat was tethered on some grass that sloped down to the water's edge. It watched us curiously as we glided by, Igor having cut the engine, enabling the silence of river and town to waft over the ship. Nothing moved and the goat remained the only sign of life as we pulled in alongside a jetty in Tsagan Aman's man-made harbour which lay beyond the houses. It was an obvious question but, even so, I couldn't help asking Ivor: 'Where is everybody?'

He responded in a tone which suggested that the answer to my question was obvious.

'There are more houses than people in this little town,' he said and then, after a pause, continued: 'All over the country, towns are shrinking as the rural population grows smaller.'

He then provided a statistic I'd read before more than once. 'There is a great grandmother who had four children; she has sixteen grandchildren and eight great grandchildren.' A sober expression blanketed his face. Of course, there was still time for her grandchildren to produce more children but this was unlikely and, what's more, missed the point of Igor's example. Whatever the reasons might be, Russia's population was in decline. And towns such as this, many often completely abandoned, were to be found all over the Federation.

Once the ship was stable, Petrov announced he would be going ashore to get some supplies. Would I like to join him, he asked?

Tsagan Aman, with its enviable location by the river, was an attractive town. A lick of paint was needed here and there, but its weathered appearance added to, rather than detracted from, its charm. The sound of cowbells could be heard as we walked past a brightly coloured temple which, equipped with oriental angles, dominated the other, less flamboyant buildings. Then, on rounding a corner, the magical atmosphere we had initially encountered disappeared, replaced by a set for a film that could have been called *Soviet Russia*.

The scene was made up of three shabby Soviet apartment blocks, which formed a semicircle which in turn formed a town square focused around a resplendent statue of Lenin. At the base of the central tower block was a shop. Petrov led us through the heavily sprung door, trying to disguise the difficulty he had opening it. He greeted the woman behind the counter with loud salutations and a big kiss on both cheeks before lifting her a good foot off the ground in a firm hug. I had already assumed that they knew each other when Petrov confirmed it.

'This is Sveta.'

He went on to explain that they stopped here every time they did this stretch of the river, which could be as many as ten times a year. Looking at Sveta with tender warmth, he said, 'Each time Sveta is here. She is my constant in an ever-changing world.'

Sveta giggled with embarrassment whilst Petrov's expression betrayed some degree of sarcasm. She then vanished out the back, giving me the opportunity to peruse the shop. It was well stocked, if a little narrow in choice, with shelves full of the edible goods free of any nutritional value that are found all over Russia: chocolate bars, crisps, fizzy drinks, cakes. There was a freezer that was empty but for two bags of frozen *pelmeni* and a five-pack of McCain pizzas. Toothpaste and soap was also available. The rest of the space was taken up with crates of bottled beer.

I asked Petrov another obvious question. 'So who buys this stuff?' Other than Sveta we had seen no sign of life since coming ashore, except for the goat. Petrov replied that many of the river-cruise boats stopped here on their way up and down the Volga.

'They buy here,' he said, 'and then sell for a profit on board.'

Sveta soon reappeared pulling a small cart loaded with boxes.

'Everything is here,' said Petrov and then, as he checked the goods he added, 'We only stop here because I'm in love with Sveta, or else,' and he winked at Sveta, 'when we've run out of beer.'

Then he winked at me. I concluded that the latter was probably the most likely reason. Yet the journey from Volgograd to Astrakhan was relatively short – by Russian standards – so maybe not.

Back on board, Petrov began to cook the evening meal for everyone in the galley. I joined the rest of the crew, except for Ron who remained on the bridge, in the poky dining room. It was the first time I'd seen everybody together, although they were clearly a tight group, a family of sorts, all very comfortable in each other's company, which made it very easy for me to feel comfortable in theirs. Vasily was a joker, with Alexander as often as not the butt of his jokes, but he took it all in good spirit, and I could tell they were both fond of one another. However, even after beer had been drunk and the obligatory vodka had joined us on the table, Igor was still very much the captain. Nobody crossed any lines with him and in return he was respectful to his crew, quite happy for them to relax knowing that they had put in plenty of hard work.

Petrov joined us to eat a fish risotto. The fish, he assured me, was Vietnamese cobbler, and my surprise prompted a depressing appraisal of the state of the fish in the Volga and the Caspian Sea further south.

THE DEATH OF CAVIAR

Caviar is the stuff of exotic living and a staple for the new Russian (and any other) elite. Unfortunately, the sturgeon, which dates back to the time of dinosaurs, is following the fast road to extinction. They, like so much directly associated with the Volga, are victims of acute fishing pressure, pollution and general destruction of their habitat. Sturgeon can grow to up to 15 feet in length, reach 100 years of age and weigh up to 2,500 pounds. However, the problem lies in their reproduction, which is often later in life; they are comparable to humans in this respect, often not getting it together until well into their twenties.

With mass fishing, they often don't get the opportunity to reproduce, and without the next generation coming through, the species is doomed. In consequence, without sturgeon producing hundreds of pounds of eggs per individual, soon there will be no more caviar for politically tumultuous countries to farm, sell on the black market and gorge themselves with.

As a second bottle of vodka made its appearance, Vasily got up and returned to work. Igor, however, was settling in, making it clear that he and Ron did shifts and this was his night off. Igor was in his fifties and, like his father before him, had been in the Soviet Navy, spending several years based in Vladivostok in the Russian Far East. With the break-up of the Soviet Union and subsequent decline of the fleet, he had offered himself out as a gun for hire.

Being highly skilled and having a deservedly solid reputation, he had found it easy to make a living piloting vessels across to Japan. Eventually, however, following his instincts, he made his way to the Volga. During the nineties he worked on other people's ships, but as soon as he had saved enough money he bought the *Lermontov* and had made a tidy living ever since. Vasily was his first and only engineer, Ron his first and only mate; such loyalty said much about the man.

The original Russian Navy was established in 1696 by Peter the Great, who is known to have said, 'A ruler that has but an army has one hand, but he who has a navy has both.' Peter's pride and joy has suffered greatly since 1991, a result of poor maintenance, low funding and inadequate training. With the demise of the Soviet Union many ships were scrapped or turned into accommodation at naval bases. More recently, however, a concerted effort has been made to re-establish the Russian Navy and its reputation around the world. In 2012 a plan was unveiled to build 51 new ships and 24 new submarines by the year 2020. Of these, 16 will be nuclear powered. The first Borei-class SSBN was accepted for service in 2013. Furthermore, in 2010 the Ukrainians extended an agreement with the Russians for them to lease the Crimean naval base facilities until 2042. However, history now suggests that they shouldn't have bothered, as in 2014 the Russians annexed the whole of the Crimean peninsula without any agreement.

Next morning there was a light drizzle. I spent the first few hours of the day up on deck, making some notes but mostly gazing out at the Russian landscape that surrounded us:

drab and mundane again but endlessly compelling. As time drifted, I took the opportunity to text Vicky news of my imminent arrival and to arrange a meeting with her and Dmitry. We had the river to ourselves for long stretches of time, until a speck would appear up ahead and, slowly but surely, evolve into a fully grown freight carrier or passenger ferry.

Meanwhile, through the rain only scruffy flatlands and rugged unkempt terrain could be seen, leading me to conclude that for those cruising this stretch of the Volga – and many people did – at least half the pleasure lay in the activities and personalities found about one's ship.

**

The hostile skies began to clear about the time Ron finished his shift on the bridge. He was replaced by a surprisingly alert and upbeat Igor, who busied himself reclaiming the bridge after Ron's shift, moving things back into place – as if his mother had been to stay. As this was going on, the blurred edge of a timid sun slowly made its appearance from behind a fluffy cloud and, somewhat less tentatively, a boat was heading towards us. This would have all been very well except for one small detail: the boat was making straight for the side of the *Lermontov* and appeared to have no intention of slowing down.

For a moment it seemed threatening. But then I realised that the oncoming boat was a tug, a relative minnow among the river-going vessels I'd seen since leaving Volgograd and, what's more, protectively attired in a black rubber tutu.

Twenty metres from the side of the *Lermontov*, the tug broke off from its course, sending up a wall of spray and white water before disappearing beyond the stern. A stickler for obeying river etiquette, Igor remained completely unfazed by this turn of events. I think I even saw the genesis of a smile on his face as he muttered the Russian equivalent of 'cabbage head'.

Moments later the tug reappeared and began a second approach towards the *Lermontov*. This time its pilot left it until his vessel was ten metres from the freight carrier before hitting a hard left on the tiller. The spray produced on this occasion splattered the bridge's window, and Igor added an adjective to his mutterings as his smile broadened into outright laughter. Shortly afterwards the tug made yet another approach, coming within inches of the *Lermontov*'s hull before the captain pulled hard on the rudder and drew to a halt with a shower of spray and an alarming screech from its engine.

The captain of the tug wore the long hair and beard of an Orthodox priest. Clearly pleased with his performance, he beamed up at the bridge like a Cheshire cat, before bellowing, 'Permission to come aboard.' The request was directed at Igor but the captain remained silent, his response made for him by Vasily, who had already lowered a rope.

The newcomer was a lively type dressed all in black. His only concession to nautical custom was the fluorescent gilet he wore and a plastic compass attached to a piece of string which hung like a medallion from his neck. Being a wide man to boot, he found it necessary to squeeze through the door and shuffle onto the bridge sideways like a crab. He greeted Igor with a firm shake of the hand followed by a friendly embrace which confirmed my suspicion that the two men knew each other.

Some banter about reckless driving followed, after which Igor introduced the man as Father Boris. He was, as I had first divined, an Orthodox priest and, more remarkably, it soon became clear that we were now in his parish.

It turned out that we had actually been in Father Boris's parish for a while. This stretched from a town just south of Volgograd all the way to Astrakhan. When Father Boris was finished with Igor he turned his attention to me, asking, 'Where are you from?' Upon hearing my response, he continued: 'Do not be worried, I am an independent man of God.' His declaration took me by surprise. I knew very little about the church in Russia, only that it was led by Patriarch Kiril and also the general view that it operated in conspiracy with the country's far from transparent rulers in the Kremlin – a symbiotic relationship that often involved not inconsiderable 'favours'.

Father Boris carried a leather satchel from which he produced a thermos flask and some tea bags. With a hot mug of tea in hand, and after having made himself comfortable in a vacant swivel chair, he asked me: 'What will you do in Astrakhan?'

This was the first time since leaving Volgograd that I had been asked anything about myself or my journey. Igor and his crew had not asked any questions. Rather they had seemed content to let me be and share a part of their lives without any greater insight into my journey. Possibly they simply didn't care, although I would like to think that their reticence was a form of courtesy. The old Soviet Union was infamous for its suspicion of strangers. Maybe, I considered, this had evolved into a weird kind of respect.

Oddly enough, once I'd told Father Boris about the wedding, his interest in me seemed to evaporate as he abruptly assumed control of the conversation. 'Marriage is good,' he said. 'God would be pleased.'

With this, he glanced up at the ceiling. I had the distinct impression that he was looking for assurance. 'After the bad days, God has arrived back in Russia. He is everywhere.'

Father Boris looked around the bridge as if to emphasise his point. I half expected God to make an appearance. 'The Russian people are good people,' he said, 'but they need guidance. For many years God's enemies had control over our great country. They are still here but there are no longer so many. It is my job to teach the people truth.'

I was slightly concerned that Boris believed I needed to be taught some truth. He continued, after having refilled his mug from the flask. 'For a long time the Russian people could only help themselves. Now we understand that we can help one another.'

Personally, I wasn't sure that I had seen much evidence of this, but I didn't want to argue with the priest. He had removed his jacket and rolled his sleeves up. Clearly he was warming to his theme, confident that in me he had found a captive audience. He wasn't wrong; I had nowhere to go. He stroked his beard whilst he repeated his assertion, 'God is everywhere, God is the river, the land. God is you. God is me.'

He gasped for air before continuing. 'We must help each other,' he said, 'giving love when we can to strangers and also to those we love.' He considered his words for a few moments before concluding. 'So marriage in Astrakhan is a good thing.'

At that point my scepticism got the better of me as thoughts of Russia's phenomenal divorce rate entered my head. According to that well-known online rag, the *European Union Times*, the number of divorces occurring in Russia has boomed in recent years. In 2012 the country actually led the world in this pursuit.

Suddenly something entirely different took hold of Father Boris as he rustled around in his bag once more and produced a litre bottle of Russian vodka.

'I think it is time to celebrate your marriage and the love that has caused it,' he announced.

The events of the next 30 minutes happened very quickly. It was as if a sudden squall had swept in off the river. China plates and cups crashed together amidst a furious whirlwind of exclamations accompanied by a soundtrack of guttural laughter. God was mentioned a lot, as was love and marriage; Putin was referred to unfavourably on several occasions. After the bottle of vodka was empty, Father Boris rose unsteadily to his feet and, seizing both my hands firmly, he asserted: 'I will now take you to my church.'

My instinctive response was to look at Igor, who, worryingly, was struggling to keep his eyes open. When I did finally catch his gaze, he simply nodded with a world-weary expression printed across his vodka-soaked face. Before I had a chance to rationally consider what dangers a visit to Father Boris's church might entail, I was slumped in the back of his tug boat, watching the shimmering river lapping against its black-rubber underside as we puttered away from the *Lermontov* towards the opposite shoreline, brilliant in the midday sun.

Father Boris's church wasn't far. It lay a short boat ride across the river in the town of Narimanov, which was 48 kilometres north-west of Astrakhan and the last significant settlement before our final destination. The town was named after an Azeri Soviet revolutionary who went by the full name of Narimanov Nariman Karbalayi Najaf oğlu – but after a bottle of vodka even Boris would have struggled to say that.

SO WHO WAS NARIMAN NARIMANOV?

Well, he was quite a guy. A teacher, medical doctor and committed Bolshevik (amongst other things), he led the first Soviet Government of Azerbaijan. Highly regarded by his revolutionary peers, he was sometimes called the 'Lenin of the East'. He wrote a large number of plays and novels and even found the time to translate Gogol's *The Government Inspector*. Lest we forget such a colossus of a man, his memorial in death is certainly the equal of his contribution in life. He has a district in Baku named after him, also a university and a metro station, an alleyway in Odessa, two streets in Volgograd and a town in Georgia, a park in Belarus... and more.

A ship similar to the *Lermontov*, in size and age, sat rusting alongside the riverbank, in front of a dilapidated building that had no windows and was partially roofless. Once Boris had fastened the tug with a thick rope to a mushroom-like cement block, we stumbled onto dry land. The ground felt spongy underfoot after being on the water for so long. Along the banks of the river fishermen could be seen perched amongst the reeds which danced in the breeze accompanied by a soft rustling sound. We followed a dusty track lined with birch trees which dissected stubbly fields.

We passed a house with a dog chained up outside furiously barking at the incumbents of a chicken coop, which stood frustratingly beyond its reach. We arrived at a house sandwiched between two other houses which Father Boris declared 'uninhabitable'. Their walls were buckled and the timber window frames had been stolen, no doubt to provide firewood during colder weather, leaving no room to doubt the priest's appraisal.

Boris led me onto the porch, the floorboards of which were rotten; an adjacent decorative window was missing its pane of glass. The porch appeared to be used as a skip; I found myself standing among rubbish – chocolate wrappers, plastic bottles and a discarded kettle.

'I'm often not here at this time of year,' Boris confirmed. 'But it is used by friends as a meeting place, and we have services here. I have an open-door policy.' As he said this the thought occurred to me that he wasn't going to have any door very soon unless he did some maintenance. Two elderly women were kneeling in the middle of the space, and, as my eyes adjusted to the light, provided by clusters of spindly candles, I was able to make out a number of icons that adorned the walls.

ICONTASTIC!

Over the past twenty years the 'artificial' aging of icons has become a widespread deception. Skilled artists will take nineteenth- and twentieth-century works and age them a few centuries – greatly increasing their value. Under present Russian law it is illegal to export icons over £100 in value, so if you do get your hands on a valuable piece outside of Russia, chances are it's been smuggled out.

Prominent among the icons present was Xenia of St Petersburg, a patron saint who spent the 45 years following the death of her husband walking the streets wearing his military uniform and no footwear. Another icon I recognised showed Boris and Gleb, the first saints to be canonised in the early federation of East Slavic tribes known as Kievan Rus'. I was busy admiring it when the two women finished muttering their prayers and, with closed eyes, climbed to their feet and respectfully kissed Father Boris on each cheek. Afterwards, the rounder of the pair passed me a candle which she lit from her own. We then received a blessing of sorts from the priest before shuffling back outside the house. The women headed in the direction of the river whilst Father Boris guided me 200 metres further down the gravel track.

Tall iron gates opened into a graveyard. Boris ushered me in with his open palm, as if having given me keys to a new car: 'Go on, it's all yours, take it for a run.'

Despite the rundown appearance of the village, the graveyard was in good shape. Avenues of neatly trimmed conifers stretched into the distance, while flowering shrubs and bushes gave the place colour. I took the keys and wandered along the avenues looking at the graves. The headstones dated from varying epochs but, although it appeared that the people buried in the graves had been well loved, I also noticed that many had been young when they died. The oldest man I found had died at the age of 50, the oldest woman, 62.

Boris, who was justly proud of the maintenance of the graveyard, which fell under his remit, remained unmoved by my comment about the relative youth of the dead.

'It is normal,' he said. 'In our country it is normal.'

At that moment, much to my surprise, several cars pulled up outside the cemetery gates. All, with the exception of a Zhiguli jeep, which looked recently polished, were splattered with mud that had dried. Crudely strapped to the roof of the jeep was a coffin, which led me to suspect that we were here by appointment and that Father Boris, clearly a man of surprises, planned to conduct a quick funeral service. However, from the bemused expression that now appeared on the priest's whiskery face, I gathered that he had no more idea than I did about what was happening. We both stood back to allow the procession of the coffin and its ten mourners into the depths of the graveyard. They passed us by as if we were invisible, while I'm sure I heard Father Boris mutter, 'Now who can that be?'

In traditional Russian Orthodox funerals, several steps must be taken before a body can be buried and the soul travel to the 'other world'. Firstly, the body has to be washed in preparation for its meeting with God (God presumably being a believer in good personal hygiene). Then it must be dressed all in white, preferably in handmade clothing which has been left slightly unfinished, 'as it belongs in the other world'. A belt should be worn which will be required during the Last Judgement. Finally, the body is laid out for three days, giving ample time for the newly dead spirit to pass on, before it is put into the coffin, referred to as the 'new living room'. Moreover, from what I can gather, the coffins are generally very comfortable, made like a bed with a pillow stuffed with birch bark and wood shavings. Mourners place objects in the coffin – items that the body might need after death, such as food, money and the deceased's favourite belongings.

The procession in the cemetery came to a halt not far from where we stood. By this point the gentle crying had become a desperate wailing which echoed alarmingly in the silent surrounds. It was a good 20 minutes until the noise petered out, the theatricals reduced to the occasional sob, whereupon one of the men present took the opportunity to speak. Oddly, although he was obviously responsible for the ceremony, he wore nothing that suggested he was a priest. When I asked Boris who he was, the latter responded with a shake of his head. 'I don't know this man,' he said, bemused, as the coffin was lowered into the ground.

Shortly afterwards the unknown man closed his book and the mourners began throwing clods of earth onto the lid of the coffin. It also sounded as if coins were being thrown, prompting Boris to say, with a smirk, 'This is to pay for the transit into the other world. Or,' he added after a pause, 'more likely to pay for a spot in the cemetery.'

Boris returned me to the ship for the final run to Astrakhan. The crew greeted me with a certain nonchalance, whilst smiles and handshakes had been reserved for Father Boris, who once again appeared to light up the ship and its crew with his presence alone.

CHAPTER NINE

A WEDDING IN ASTRAKHAN

*'All life passes like a fast flowing river and
how strange to see that happiness increases
this speed! Yes a happy life passes faster.'*
Mehmet Murat Ildan

Astrakhan features in Andrey Kurkov's book *The Good
Angel of Death*. This had been my only exposure to the
city until Vicky had brought it onto my radar. It was first
mentioned by travellers in the early thirteenth century as
Xacitarxan, burnt to the ground by the armies of Tamerlane
(warlord and all-round imperialist) in 1395. The ruins from
this medieval settlement were found by archaeologists some
twelve kilometres upstream from present-day Astrakhan in

the 1960s. In the seventeenth century the city was groomed as the gateway to the Orient, with many merchants from Armenia, Persia and India settling in the town, giving it the cosmopolitan character which it still has to this day.

The city also gave its name to a popular hat to be found all over Eurasia. The Astrakhan hat is made from the fur of the Karakul breed of sheep – actually, and somewhat offputtingly, more often than not from the fur of aborted lamb foetuses. In the USSR, the triangular hat became popular amongst Politburo members and it was common for leaders to appear in public wearing it. It gained prestige among the Communist Party leaders as it was previously an obligatory parade accessory for the Czarist and Soviet generals, underlining their high political status. In the Soviet Union the Astrakhan also gained the nickname 'the pie hat' as it had a close resemblance to the traditional Russian pie.

SOME FAMOUS WEARERS OF THE ASTRAKHAN
- Leonid Brezhnev
- Hamid Karzai
- Eddie Murphy

I had 24 hours before I was due to meet with Dmitry and Vicky. Having disembarked the good ship *Lermontov*, I drifted down dusty roads soaking up the unique and unexpectedly urbane atmosphere of the city that took over from two other imperial capitals, Saray and Itil, as the region's most prosperous settlement – a result of its position on the Caspian Sea and its location on the Silk Road.

Joining the Red Embankment that ran from the Volga River, I passed beautiful nineteenth-century pastel houses. One of these houses was now used as a hospital, and had been the home of the merchant Shelekhov, identifiable by the statue of a woman on the roof.

Legend has it that at night the statue comes to life and walks along the corridors of the hospital. Past patients have claimed to have heard moans and weeping. The story goes that after the early death of Shelekhov's daughter, from tuberculosis at the age of 17, the merchant had found it difficult to remain in the house, unable to sleep. However, one night Shelekhov fell into a deep sleep and his daughter came to him with hope shining in her eyes. She took the opportunity to ask her father to turn their mansion into a place to help sick people, a place where she would stay and protect them. So he did just that. In 1922 the house was turned into a hospital and a statue of Shelekhov's daughter placed on the roof.

On a narrow street parallel to the Red Embankment I arrived at the heavy wooden door of the Beka Hotel, beside which a mare and her foal grazed on sporadic patches of grass. Finding a large reception area, I was immediately deluged by the familiar smell of cigarette smoke. The source of the redolence was perhaps the short stocky man at the opposite end of the space, who stood with both arms stretched above his head, as if being frisked. Initially I thought he might be exercising. But closer inspection revealed that he was in fact straightening a picture of a woman riding a horse. A cigarette hung precariously from his mouth, the ash defying all laws of gravity, while in an ashtray that rested on the edge of a counter another cigarette burned. There was, curiously, nobody else in sight.

Having stood at the counter for several minutes, I cleared my throat gently; the smoke from the ashtray spiralling into my face made my gesture almost genuine. The stocky man continued his adjustments, while my attention was drawn to loud footsteps coming from the stairway to my left. The noise seemed to fire the man into life. No words were uttered; he simply hurried to the desk where, opening a drawer, he extracted a form which he offered to me with the genesis of a smile, pointing with his nose to a pen before glancing back over his shoulder at the still crooked picture. I filled out the laborious form which required, among other things, my four previous addresses in the UK and the occupations of all my direct family.

'Breakfast is between seven and ten, on the third-floor dining room.'

My host spoke good English – he just apparently preferred not to. 'No food after ten,' he stressed.

He then handed me a substantial iron key attached to a lump of metal the shape and size of a light bulb. I certainly wouldn't be walking off with it. Our brief exchange over, my host lit up another cigarette and returned to his picture. I followed the stairway up to the fourth floor; copies of works by the artists Davit Kakabadze, Lado Gudiashvili and Shalva Kikodze lined the walls. The first of whom was something of a jack of all artistic trades; as well as painting he was handy with a camera and also lent his hand to set design, having in the 1930s collaborated with Kote Marjanashvili (the Georgian dramaturge) at his theatre in Kutaisi on several productions.

Gudiashvili also had his hands in several pies, known not only as a painter but also as a practising monumentalist. Unfortunately, however, his work in this particular field wasn't so well received; in 1946, having painted the Kashveti Church in Tbilisi, he was sacked from his job at the city's academy and then expelled from the Communist Party for his trouble.

Kikodze, on the other hand, sensibly stuck with painting.

Highlighting the paintings, a golden chandelier, suspended by heavy-link chains and boasting a pale figurine of the Virgin Mary, adorned each landing. We could have been in the holiest of churches. Upon arriving at the fourth floor, I entered a corridor and passed what appeared to be the laundry room, a TV or radio crackling within. The corridor was dimly lit, but not so dimly, alas, that it managed to disguise the nauseating turquoise paint on the walls. I counted off the room numbers all the way to the end, and had the key in the lock when suddenly I heard, 'Shto, shto.'

Bracing myself, I looked towards the source. It stood by the door of the laundry room I had passed moments earlier: a tall and proud-looking woman, wearing thick woolly socks pulled up to the knees that concealed a set of calves at least a foot wide. A look of disgruntled desperation grew across her ruddy complexion as she moved ever closer. She was straining noticeably under the pace, hindered by her now distorted yelps of 'Shto, shto', that versatile Russian word again, which can mean anything from 'Who are you and what do you want?' to 'Alright there, haven't seen you for a while'. I found myself hypnotised by the vision steaming towards me, my hand glued to the key as my feet were to the floor. Then she was upon me; in one blinding flash of movement she drew from under her arm a tightly packed bundle of sheets, which she plunged with considerable force into my unsuspecting stomach. I winced as the wind left my body like steam from a pressure cooker.

My initial impression was that I had been given the storeroom. Three mahogany chests of drawers were piled one above each other behind the door; two wardrobes leant insouciantly against the right-hand wall; wooden slats lay indiscriminately on the floor. In amongst the debris sat an iron bed, with a liberal distribution of springs, with a loosely rolled mat rested upon them.

Opposite the door, on the outside wall, was a porthole window fronted by metal bars. Having already made my mind firmly up that under no circumstances would I be troubling the laundry lady, I decided, what the hell, I had a bed (of sorts), and after rolling out the mat I actually found it to be surprisingly comfortable. I lay down on the bed and gazed at the ceiling which was splattered with nicotine stains. A lamp dangled from a scrawny wire protected by a cloudy plastic lampshade. The lampshade darkened towards the base, and, as I continued to stare, I realised that I was looking at a pile of dead flies – bluebottles there since the previous summer.

AN AWKWARD HOTEL BREAKFAST INCIDENT

A young guy sat at the table stuffing Sugar Puffs into his mouth. At the other end of the table a couple of more mature age were engaged in a fierce discussion, glancing around intermittently to see if anyone else was interested in their conversation. Even if it's questionable that dogs do in fact look like their owners, there is certainly some truth in a person looking like their partner – perhaps it's the narcissistic hunt for an image of oneself, or perhaps the acquisition of characteristics over time. Either way, this particular couple were born to be together. Come to think of it, there was a strong chance that they had been born together.

My slice of cheese found its way onto an antiquated slice of bread. Together, unfortunately, the two components proved quite inedible. The younger man rose from the table offering a parting shot, 'There is much to see in Astrakhan – you must see the kremlin.' He repeated his recommendation as he vanished into the corridor still chewing on the Sugar Puffs, his words confirming to me, if there had been any doubt, that I was indeed a tourist in Russia.

A few moments later another man appeared at the door, where he paused to survey the room. He stood about six feet tall and had dark features.

'I've been here a week and only once have I been in time for the cereal,' he said. 'You would think they were trying to discourage tourists, or kill them off all together,' he chuckled.

'You been here long?'

'Where – Astrakhan?'

'Yes, Astrakhan, this hotel, Russia.'

'One night covers the first two.'

'Any plans this morning?' he continued.

I was reminded that I was due to meet with Dmitry at midday.

'So where are you from?' I asked, aware that I had simply labelled him as a tourist. He took a long inhalation of air, as if preparing to dive underwater.

'I'm Circassian.' He paused to gauge whether or not I knew what he was talking about. 'The indigenous people of the north-west Caucasus. You've heard of the Caucasian War, yeah?'

I nodded my confirmation.

'Well, the Circassians were cleansed from their own homeland by the victorious Russians.' His face had taken on a rather more serious expression. 'The expulsions were mostly complete by 1867 but still continued into the 1870s – the first modern ethnic cleansing and genocide.'

My companion looked closely to see my reaction, having intended to shock me. He had and I wasn't sure the best way to respond. So I didn't and he continued.

'It was an unknown number of people but perhaps hundreds of thousands. The Russian army rounded up the "mountain people", driving them from their villages to ports on the Black Sea where they awaited ships. They had a choice – they could resettle in the Ottoman Empire or in Russia, far from their old lands. Few chose Russia. Many perished on the boats.'

If I'd been half asleep before, I was awake now. His eyes bored into me as he appeared increasingly angry, as if he'd wanted to get this off his chest for a while and he now had the perfect opportunity to dump it on me. Meanwhile, I considered how easy it would be to change the subject to the weather.

THE CIRCASSIAN GENOCIDE

Czar Nicholas endorsed the plans to 'cleanse the land of hostile elements' in 1864. Although the Circassians were the main victims of the expulsions, other peoples were also affected: about 80 per cent of the Ingush left Ingushetia in 1865, and many Chechens were also evicted from their lowland homes. By the end of the resettlement over 400,000 Circassians as well as 200,000 Abkhazians had fled to Turkey.

It meant considerable hardships for all the survivors, and many eventually died of starvation; many contemporary Turks descended from the Circassians don't eat fish in memory of all those who died in the Black Sea crossing – a gesture that, if extended to the Volga region, might help the dwindling sturgeon population.

After breaking free of my intense breakfast companion, I went for a walk in the district north of the train station to shake off the gloom. It's considered one of the city's more affluent areas, despite the neighbourhood being built over the graves of those killed in the 1930s purges, so perhaps not the best place to cast off the catatonia of breakfast. I walked past the neoclassical State University, once a school for the children of nobles; this beautiful building dominated the mouth of Ulitsa Lenina, a tree-lined boulevard. Students mingled, as if at a party, around the gates to the university, chatting and laughing, swigging from cans of drink under the gentle sun. I continued along the wide road lined with apartment blocks and a scattering of restaurants; outlets for expensive products such as electrical goods sat alongside branded coffee shops and pharmacies.

As I walked I remembered the views of a sixteenth-century merchant. Anthony Jenkinson was sent to the city to explore the practicalities of a land route to China. He wasn't very impressed. He arrived in 1558 and said Astrakhan was:

Most destitute and barren of wood and pasture, and the ground will bear no corn. The air is most infected, by reason (as I suppose) of much fish, and especially sturgeon, by which only the inhabitants live, having great scarcity of flesh and bread. They hung their fish in their streets and houses to dry for their provisions which causeth such abundance of flies.

Nowadays, fortunately, the smell wasn't too bad; but as I glanced down the narrow streets it was still possible to see a catch of fish drying alongside T-shirts, bedsheets and underwear on the wrought-iron balconies of the houses. I was grateful that the flies were still asleep. The temperature in the summer months often reached as high as 50°C, so the flies certainly would be along later.

One benefit of such extremes of temperature is the size of the tomatoes that are produced – big and succulent. In a nice touch, the locals add an 'a' to the masculine Russian word for tomato, making it feminine, not due to any physical comparison but simply because the tomatoes are so wonderful. The area surrounding the city is known as 'Russia's kitchen garden' due to the abundance of locally grown fruit and vegetables, which include watermelons and aubergines. Another benefit of the high temperatures is the brilliant burnt colours of the leaves on the trees. Yellows and rusty oranges merge with browns and a deep and evocative red.

The kremlin was unquestionably the city's architectural highlight. Its green and gold domes, rising above the whitewashed and crenellated walls, could be glimpsed down streets and alleys from all over the city centre. There was also a number of mosques in the city and plenty of new buildings, not least the hulking brown and blue Gazprom offices in the historical 'centre', soon to be the recipient of Igor's well-travelled flat-packs.

These offices weren't exactly the highlight of Astrakhan, but their existence was certainly revealing. Money from this state-owned gas giant financed the reconstruction of the city's 1.8 kilometres of waterfront embankment in 2008. Furthermore, Gazprom employs five thousand of the city's residents, who are shuttled in and out each day on company buses. So, one way or another, Gazprom appears to have Astrakhan in its not inconsiderable pocket.

A COUPLE OF THINGS YOU MIGHT LIKE TO KNOW ABOUT GAZPROM

1. It is short for *Gazovaya Promyshlennost*, which means 'Gas Industry'.
2. In 2011 the company was responsible for some 17 per cent of global gas production.

After a couple of kilometres the buildings either side of Lenina seemed to get lower and lower, and the trees, which had been thick at the eastern end of the street, suddenly became less dense, having gradually receded like the hair of a balding man. It ended in a roundabout with little roads leading off to nowhere. It didn't matter because the main point of interest was the park, which was now visible on the slope of a ridge, commencing impressively at the foot of a wide stone staircase.

Astrakhan often offered up tantalising suggestions of space with glimpses of distant flatlands and then mountains at various vantage points around the city. To escape the claustrophobia of the city itself, I continued along the ornate lamppost-lined boulevard, past a multi-coloured children's play area, and began climbing the increasingly steep steps, slowly enough to read all the messages that had been painted on the concrete. These ranged from 'Queen is God' (I assumed this was a reference to the band) to 'Sveta and Petr forever', although, towards the top, these pleasant sentiments gave way to the far more menacing 'kill Sakashvili', as if perhaps the steep climb had got the better of somebody's civil nature (although, then again, it's doubtful anyone would have the stomach for murder after such an ascent; the breathtaking views of the distant tower blocks and beyond were enough to numb any festering frustrations, at least temporarily).

After the 20-minute climb I had to sit down for a few minutes under the shadow of the colossal statue that kept a dominant watch over the park, the memorial of glory. At the base of the statue, crumbled bricks had been sculpted together to form makeshift fire pits, overflowing with ash. The obligatory polythene bags littered the uneven terrace.

Having caught my breath, I scrambled up an even steeper path through brambles, occasionally stopping to enjoy the increasingly hypnotic views of rooftops and Astrakhan's surrounding undulations. Clambering out of the now particularly thick undergrowth I stumbled over to an oversized garden shed, which was a cable car terminal. Brief scrutiny revealed the cable car option hadn't been available for several years if not decades. A lake was nearby, and back in the days of Soviet yore I imagined it would have been a very popular weekend excursion. Restaurants and boat hire were still available. However, on this particular Tuesday, late in the morning, I walked into a post-apocalyptic scene: litter underfoot, upturned plastic tables and chairs, cigarette butts carpeting the sandy gravel. I considered the 'lake', a man-made creation with murky brown water, and quickly dispelled any notion that there were indeed turtles living within its dirty depths – as its name 'Turtle Lake' tried to suggest.

The main reason for climbing to the top of the park was to see the remnants of a Museum of Ethnography, which, lying some three kilometres further north, displayed folk architecture and craftwork from all regions of the ex-Soviet Union.

Located on a large hillside to the west of the city, the museum was essentially a historic village comprising buildings from all over Russia. Included in the collection were flat-roofed stone houses from eastern Georgia, watchtowers from Dagestan and Chechnya, Kakhetian wineries, Karelian water mills and an early Christian 'Sioni' basilica from Kiev. I soon ran out of time, such were the distances between the exhibits, but it was quite an amazing place and I more than once told myself that I would be going back. However, I didn't want to be late for Dmitry.

***

I had told Dmitry that I was more than happy to make my own arrangements regarding accommodation. He wouldn't hear of it. Unfortunately, the flat he temporarily shared with Vicky would be full with family descending for the wedding, but, he said, there would be somewhere close by that would be more than adequate.

I had expected to see him at the station, where we had arranged to rendezvous, so it was something of a surprise when a formidable-looking man firmly grabbed my arm and barked 'Come!'. He then proceeded to tug me through the crowds and out onto the taxi-lined street, his formidable presence enabling him to part the crowd like Moses the sea, my rucksack following obediently at arm's length, bouncing off the platform and clipping more than a few submissive onlookers. I was grateful to be in such apparently capable and certainly firm hands.

We headed towards a dirty Lada parked awkwardly on the collapsed pavement. Cramped introductions over, a language barrier clearly in place, I felt completely at ease in the close company of another Igor and his Lada, the strong aroma of leather coming from his jacket acting as a mild tranquiliser when fused with the smell of tobacco. Igor could have taken me anywhere. As it happens, he took me approximately 200 metres around the corner from the station and, whilst doing so, managed to clear his small Soviet runaround of all the rubbish it had accumulated over what might have been many months. With the small leverage he was able to get with his spare hand, he reached around the car for empty Fanta bottles, beer cans, cigarette packets, chocolate wrappers and plastic cups, and threw them through his open window and onto the street. Shortly afterwards we came to a halt outside a tall, time-weary Soviet tower block.

TWO UKRAINIAN PROVERBS ABOUT LOVE

- Love well, whip well.
- If you marry a young woman, make sure your friends stay outside.

As I had never been aware of Vicky ever displaying any particular religious leanings, I put the wedding's Christian veneer down to Dmitry's desires. Vicky confirmed what I had suspected; she was living with and marrying a Ukrainian and, as the wedding was taking place in a Ukrainian church, she believed the least she could do was to go along with it. Not least as I was the only representative on her side making the journey to Astrakhan. But I'm not sure she had realised how very traditional her in-laws were. 'You know I'm not averse to a bit of folk music and some silly dancing,' she had said. A large number of the Astrakhan region's residents are Orthodox, while there are some Muslims and a not insignificant number of Catholics. More surprisingly, there are a significant number of neo-pagans.

Later that day, a meeting had been organised for all those involved in the wedding – friends and family who had travelled to be there – giving everyone an opportunity to get to know one another before the big day. I got a lift with Igor to a restaurant not far from the port. It was late afternoon, the hour reflected by the sun making its descent, when we arrived at the wooden-slat two-storey building. The ground floor was given over to the restaurant. Vicky was at the door meeting guests, with her big smile and warm rosy cheeks, looking considerably more relaxed than the occasion possibly demanded. We hugged for what seemed like a long time, as I melted into the safe warmth of the embrace, for the first time feeling like I'd really arrived. She suggested we 'go and meet the girls', pointing over to a large table besieged by a group of ladies all comfortably in middle age and, judging by the guffaws and shrieks, all comfortably working their way through the vodka. Igor led the way and after a few words of introduction we were both warmly welcomed into the bosom of the *svashky* – the traditional name for the women's choir.

First impressions suggested that this particular *svashky* had absolutely no intention of fulfilling their traditional role; clearly, theirs was a celebration that had been going on for some time. They seemed interested in me, wanting to know specifically why I chose to attend such an event with Igor as a companion and thus the peculiarity of the complaint that I must be suffering from. Introductions out of the way, the most vocal of the group, a woman named Olga, dragged me onto the dance floor.

This proved a challenge I was only just up to meeting. Olga had stamina, whirling, flinging, carrying and dragging me around the dance floor for a good hour or more, much of which was spent trying to avoid – or failing to avoid – crashing into other dancers. The dance of choice seemed to be a crude variant on a jive, lots of hip twisting and arm waving above the head. Well at least that's what Olga was doing. One couple appeared to be waltzing and another were successfully pulling off what looked like a Cossack-themed knees-up. Igor looked on, clearly enjoying the company of seven bawdy women. By the time I had collapsed back into a chair, Vicky and her bridegroom were ready to address the assembled crowd.

Dmitry spoke in Ukrainian, which I didn't understand, but his gently flowing oration had the audience transfixed and it was easy to conclude he was a much loved, and loving, man. Vicky stood by his side, beaming whilst hanging off his every word; she was clearly very much in love and the aura they both created was quite infectious. Eventually it was Vicky's turn to speak; she spoke in faltering Russian, which I was impressed by. She had the choir girls rolling around in hysterics and, once into her stride, gave the impression that she could have continued all night.

She didn't, of course, as eventually Eugene, the father-in-law to be, appeared and began toasting. Fresh reserves of vodka arrived on the tables as he kicked off with a toast to the 'young lovers... an example to the world'. He then proceeded to toast... well, just about anything and everything: the Caspian Sea, heaven, children and flowers, the sun and the moon, and on it went. I even think that Buckingham Palace got a mention – but in what capacity I couldn't say.

Raucous the evening certainly was, euphoric and joyous too, though memorable I can't be sure. However, one thing's for certain: it was the start of several days of celebration the likes of which I'd never seen and on health grounds alone would be glad not to see again for a while. During my stay in Astrakhan I was surrounded by people hungrily eating up every last drop of life, people who found very little to complain about.

The bridegroom being Ukrainian, it was no surprise that relations had made the journey from all over the Federation to be at the wedding. Some of the distances other guests had travelled made my own trip pale into insignificance. However, as the sole representative of Vicky's 'old' life back in England, I felt that my journey was particularly significant. Dmitry's brother and sister had come from Novosibirsk in Siberia. When asked what he did in Siberia, Dmitry's brother gruffly replied in a voice deep as a well, 'I work in oil.' He didn't expand upon this and had such a cagey manner about him I suspected that perhaps 'work in oil' was a cover for something else. His beautiful sister cleared up any such suspicions by proudly adding that Piotr was 'important in a company operating all around the world'. Suitably impressed, I didn't press either of them further, just settled in to the warmth of the company they provided.

During a conversation with the sister, Natalia, I experienced an overpowering sense of bemusement – brought on when she used the word 'desert' whilst describing the region around Astrakhan.

'Of course most of the area is desert and there is the largest *barakhan* [sand dune] in the Federation,' she said.

It was nothing new for a Russian to claim to have the largest anything. Russians live and think in a world of superlatives, but I was more than a little surprised that any Russian could claim to have a desert on their doorstep. There weren't any deserts in Russia, were there? Kurkov hadn't mentioned any deserts; in the only novel I'd read to include Astrakhan as a setting, there had been plenty of sand dunes in Kazakhstan – they had provided the perfect setting for the baby-milk-powder-fuelled hallucinogenic escapades of the novel's main characters – but none in Russia. In all my travels in Russia I had never heard a word uttered about desert, let alone seen one. I was incredulous.

'There aren't any deserts in Russia, surely?' I said.

Natalia gave me a look that said, 'And what would you know?'

I had certainly heard some tall stories whilst in Russia but I did think the creation of a whole desert was pushing it a bit. Also Natalia didn't really seem the tall-story-weaving type. This desert, therefore, I would have to see for myself, and I would. But first, the wedding day.

TWO UKRAINIAN PROVERBS WITH NO LOVE ASSOCIATION

- A friendly word is better than a heavy cake.
- Wisdom is in the head, not in the beard.

The day of the wedding arrived. The steps leading up to the church were packed with people decked out in their finery, complemented by the magnolia backdrop of the building. It was a magnificent church in the classical style, not far from the city's central gardens, resplendent with a cupola shaped like a tin-pot helmet.

Once the huge mass of people, amoeba-like, had seeped inside, it was impossible to not be hypnotised by the imposing interior; the roof seemed to rise all the way to heaven, while the dual altar, though a mere 20 metres away, looked impossibly distant. A cooling draught tickled the back of my neck. I felt privileged to be inside such a beguiling building. There was much to look at as the assembled crowd waited with a palpable air of excitement for the bride to arrive.

Dmitry stood upright and confident by the altar, seemingly unfazed by the occasion (I felt anxious and all I had to do was watch). Eventually the large, intricately carved wooden door swung teasingly open and Vicky appeared, looking like a picture, ready to make the slow walk down the aisle. At this point the *svashky* kicked in; the collective I had met the day before had been a mere shadow of what now burst into song. They were in fine voice: they might have looked a bit rough after the excess of the previous day but, complemented by the church's pure acoustics, they gave an angelic audio assault.

The priest spoke through a microphone attached to his collar. He was a heavily bearded man with thick brown hair in a ponytail down to his waist; his appearance added to the drama, although his gentle voice was, I thought, incongruous with his bear-like appearance. The ceremony was relatively brief and proceeded in Ukrainian, and, understanding none of it, I let the soft sense of the ritual wash over me, the power of the sentiment working its magic. As I looked on, soaking up the atmosphere, I couldn't help but think how mundane and dull marriage would be after such a momentous beginning. Yet, perhaps this spectacular launch would carry it through, acting as a grand springboard that would propel the lovers into a carefree life of love and happiness, and many children. These were the priest's words, not mine.

After the spoken part of the ceremony was done with, it was time to sing and then sing some more. There were only three songs, Ukrainian hymns to be specific, but they were three very long Ukrainian hymns. Eventually many of the voices became hoarse, whereupon the congregation filed up to the altar to greet the married couple and sign the register. The formalities dealt with, the guests broke ranks and so began an orgy of hugging and kissing; everyone got a turn, so that it resembled a feel-good hugging workshop, twenty or so minutes of embracing and being embraced by complete strangers. To my surprise I found it compelling therapy, especially as, by the end, my cheeks were damp with all the wet lips that had been plunged onto them.

At the same time I now felt at one with my fellow guests. Indeed, if it hadn't existed before, there was now a strong air of union amongst us. I didn't want it to stop but the departure of Dmitry and Vicky brought proceedings to a close, and the church was gradually vacated to the sound of the choir singing Beatles variations, which went some way to firing the starting pistol for the party that was to follow. The business part of the day was now over.

A VOLGA DISCLAIMER

The accuracy of the following event is dubious but to the best of my recollection how things unfolded. I have since, however, heard some revisionist theories that are probably best omitted.

Outside the church several cars had been laid on for family. Igor and I would follow in the Lada. The restaurant was in fact only just around the corner but it took much longer to get there than the five minutes it should have taken. First, the entire wedding convoy was obliged to drive around the city blowing horns, yelling from windows, even throwing things at people in the street – well, Igor certainly did. Having just been married gave you free rein on the roads of Astrakhan, and normal road-safety-conscious citizens temporarily went nuts, all driving inhibitions simply thrown to the wind.

All this, I thought, came quite instinctively to Igor, but when I saw Eugene ride up onto the pavement and splash a passer-by with what looked like wine, I was indeed surprised. At one point the car directly in front slowed right down, ribbons flowing from its wing mirrors, and a pedestrian leapt onto the bonnet and was carried along for some fifty metres. The wedding was now being shared with the whole city, the joy of the occasion spreading beyond the participants.

We passed the peachy exterior of the Central Hotel before gliding down towards the port. Astrakhan had become an unofficial Grand Prix circuit, a bit like Monaco for a weekend in April, only there were no safety barriers and, certainly, none of the residents had been informed.

We hurtled past the State Theatre of Opera and Ballet, nearly crashing straight through the Pushkin Monument. A large crowd outside the City Hall opposite cheered as the convoy swerved snake-like past one of the city's proudest features. On we motored, the grip I had on the dashboard getting firmer and firmer, past the splendour of the monument to Peter the Great, before changing direction and heading out in the direction of the seaport again.

Pumped up with adrenalin, with more than a little relief I clambered out of Igor's car onto terra firma. The convoy broke ranks and scattered chaotically across a wasteland car park situated in the shadow of the cranes of the docks nearby. It was the perfect setting for a gangland murder.

Friends and family sat down around a long, heavy oak dining table. I proceeded to eat more caviar than I had ever eaten before, which wasn't difficult as I had never before eaten caviar, and the way things were heading there soon wouldn't be much left to eat. Eugene took his position as master of ceremonies at the head of the table, and firmly announced in Ukrainian, '*Mbl dobry vremya*', which roughly translates as 'May we all have a good time'. He followed this predictably with a toast to the bride and groom.

Next, 'To friendship', Eugene bellowed, and at this point any of the group were given the opportunity to add their own variant on the theme. It wasn't compulsory, of course, but it's important to engage every other round or so, and probably best to get your addition noticed early on before things got too outlandish. Piotr was no fool and, wanting to make his words count, got in early: 'To new friends and old.' Brief and to the point, altogether very efficient work, I thought, whilst cursing him for nabbing sentiments I'd thought of delivering.

Vicky was no stranger to the art of toasting either and was quick to follow up with, 'Here's to friends we've yet to meet.' I wasn't so sure about that one; still, it was punchy and seemed to hit the spot as everyone clinked glasses and slugged wine, whilst at the same time echoing, 'Yet to meet.'

Igor was next to throw words of wisdom into the mix. 'To all the people who do not want to be your friend.' Umm, slightly lost in translation? There were a few bemused faces, but glasses were again chinked along with a chorus of something indecipherable, sounding like, 'I don't want to be your friend.'

After a short lull Eugene was back on his feet, chomping at the bit and, I don't think it would be unfair to say, frothing at the mouth with a new toast topic. Such was the believed complexity of the sentiment being offered, he first roared out the toast in Ukrainian which Natalia more meekly translated for us. I'm sure some of the sentiment was again lost in translation but the gist was, 'To the sun in the sky for sustaining our world and sustaining our human spirits.' Eugene was a great hulk of a man. It seemed unlikely that such hippy-dippy words should come from his warrior-like person, but we all went with it, while an ever-watchful Jeeves stood by, quick to fill any glasses that had become depleted of wine.

I wasn't going to miss my chance this time and put forward with probably a little too much enthusiasm, 'Here's to all the mountains that give us strength,' whereupon Vicky gave me a look as if to say, 'Yeah, whatever.' I self-consciously slugged from my glass, while Igor quickly followed up with, 'To all our enemies…'

Nobody seemed to bat an eyelid at his blatant deviation from the theme. The sister-in-law quickly got us back on track with, 'Here's to all the beautiful birds.' Igor hadn't apparently finished, '… even the Russians.'

Now surely nobody was going to swallow that, but no, even that got a volley of chinks. And on it went. Traditionally the topic of the fifth round of toasts should be the fondly remembered departed and Eugene, not wanting to stray from tradition, gave us all something to think about: 'Here's to all the dead people.' It was a little indelicately put, but we all got the picture.

The pace was slowing down by this stage, so Piotr had a few moments to consider his development on this theme, and without being overcritical I think he could have been slightly more original. 'And to all our loved ones, who can't be with us anymore.' It didn't matter; by the fifth round of toasts, thanks to all the alcohol involved, I wasn't convinced anybody was paying much attention.

One of the necessary skills of the MC is to read his audience, not only for stamina but more importantly for enthusiasm, and I think that after round seven he sensed a decline in both so wrapped it up with a traditional toast to finish events. Thus Eugene blasted out one last time (at least until the next spontaneous eruption of toasts, which was likely to happen any time), 'To God and all his love.' Chink, chink, chink.

Vicky followed this up quite unnecessarily with, 'To God and all his dove.' Dmitry then seemed to feel the need to contribute, but he simply managed, 'God.' As I emptied my glass on the fourth chink of the God round, all I could manage was, 'Oh my god,' before slumping back into my chair and considering how easy and inconspicuous it would be to drag myself back to the apartment. Needless to say, the rest of the evening was something of a haze, although noisy, even boisterous, concluding with much dancing... I think.

* * *

The following day Vicky and Dmitry began their honeymoon. Dmitry had indicated that the first day would most probably be devoted to exchanging toasts with a variety of people. Vicky had been somewhat clearer, saying that the day would be spent avoiding alcohol, even to the point of running away from those people wielding it, as for months their pending wedding had served as a justification for large amounts of boozing in whatever company they had found themselves in. As for me personally, on the back of my earlier conversation with Natalia, I would spend the first day of the couple's honeymoon with a sore head in Russia's foremost 'desert'.

Piotr had jumped at the opportunity of getting out of the city and doing a spot of toasting himself, with me and Natalia in tow, while Natalia was keen to prove to me that there were parts of Russia with lunar landscapes – I had noticed, however, that since the subject had first come up, the 'desert' landscape of the Astrakhan oblast had down-shifted to 'semi-desert'. Whether it resembled the Sahara or just a blotchy bit of scrubland, I saw it as a fitting conclusion not only to the wedding celebration but also to my entire Volga trip. As we bounced along, our hangovers getting the better of idle chit-chat, I enjoyed the irony of concluding my journey in a desert with not a drop of water in sight.

The jeep Piotr had acquired from someone he described as 'Oh, just some relative I've never met before'. We passed the Persil-white kremlin with its green cupolas clashing with the pale blue Caspian sky and the Prechistinsky Gate or bell tower with its 80-metre silhouette visible all around the city. Before long we had left the outskirts of the city behind, eventually picking up a narrow sandy track that climbed a gradual incline, dividing the stubbly green shrubs and bushes of the semi-desert on either side. Then, after several hours of driving, we arrived at a small red-brick bungalow which sat as the gatehouse to the vast expanse of nothingness that sprawled beyond. The emptiness stretched all the way to the horizon and on into the pale blue of the distant sky. Waving an excited finger, Natalia pointed out that somewhere in all that bleakness lay the border with Dagestan.

Piotr pulled up alongside the bungalow, which could have been part of a set for a western, in front of which three colourfully dressed children stood hypnotised by our arrival. They froze, mouths wide open, for several moments before performing a synchronised jump into the air and running off at speed.

'We used to come up here as children,' Piotr said with a longing tone in his voice, his childhood now as distant as the back-of-beyond we found ourselves looking at. 'This house was always empty then, derelict. It had no roof and all the walls were crumbling. We called it the ruined castle.'

He looked over at Natalia for some acknowledgement of their shared history. She produced a smile that required no words of clarification. My own thoughts drifted back to the years I'd spent with Vicky building castles out of straw bales and those contented summers of our childhood. It was, I reflected wearily, a world away from Astrakhan and Russia and from growing up into the lives we now had. I reflected on how fortunate I was to still be part of Vicky's life (and Dmitry's), grateful for their union which had gifted me something very special, an adventure that would now become part of my life and stay with me forever. And all because I didn't have any business acumen. If I had even had the slightest clue about selling holidays, it's fairly safe to say Vicky would never have met Dmitry. I had failed in creating a successful business, but I had played my part in creating something without comparison, the best thing in the world and the only thing that will ever really matter... love. I had met many people over the last few days; but more than that, over the past months I'd glimpsed the lives of many more. Vicky's wedding had allowed me to see the heart of Russia, a Russia removed from newspaper headlines and hearsay.

Piotr climbed out of the jeep and walked over to the bungalow. Getting no reply to his knock on the door, he vanished inside. The bungalow had a roof now and was in relatively good repair, with solid brick walls and a wooden door. Moreover, the interior showed signs of having once been loved. A wooden table with four stools sat in the middle. On the air hung a mouldy smell of damp. Piotr suggested that the place was probably used by herders as an overnight bolthole. Natalia confirmed this as she placed the leftovers box on the table and started to empty out the contents: two loaves of rye bread, four bottles of champagne (and three glasses) and five medium-sized tins of caviar.

In the unlit hut, natural light came from a small window which offered a view out over the semi-desert scrubland.

'The area is quite unique,' Piotr continued. 'Nowhere else can you find the Volga, only kilometres away, a desert and camels.'

He waited for my reaction to the last bit. I thought he was joking but, as he spoke, a camel with its Kazakh herder passed by the window. After it had gone we all took a seat around the table and, with glasses charged in the middle of our Russian desert, we drank a toast to Vicky and Dmitry Spiritov and to all the happy times that lay ahead of them. Just as I had reached the end of my journey on the Volga, their journey had just begun.

ONE STEPPE BEYOND
Across Russia in a VW Camper

Thom Wheeler

ISBN: 978 84953 156 6
Paperback
£8.99

Travelling across the former Soviet Union is a challenge at the best of times – but in a dilapidated VDub... that's got to be plain daft... hasn't it?

A chance job offer at a timber yard in Estonia gives Thom and his old pal Jo a taste for the unknown. So when Uncle Tony asks them to drive to Vladivostok for another job, they can't think of a good reason why not.

The result is a classic caper across the former Soviet Union in Max, a rusty old VW camper. Knowing little of the language or the geography ahead, they embark on probably the longest commute ever, encountering corrupt officials, film star mechanics and over-friendly gangsters. Far off the tourist trail, they bear witness to the collapse of one nation and the birth of a new one during the free-for-all that was Russia in the nineties.

'This engaging tale will be an inspiration for anyone who's ever daydreamed about abandoning the humdrum and hitting the road'

John Mole, author of *I Was a Potato Oligarch*

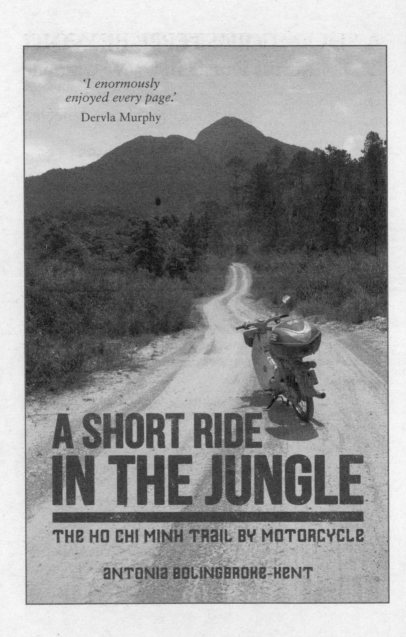

A SHORT RIDE IN THE JUNGLE
The Ho Chi Minh Trail by Motorcycle

Antonia Bolingbroke-Kent

ISBN: 978 84953 543 4
Paperback
£9.99

The Ho Chi Minh Trail is one of the greatest feats of military engineering in history. But since the end of the Vietnam War much of this vast transport network has been reclaimed by jungle, while remaining sections are littered with a deadly legacy of unexploded bombs. For Antonia, a veteran of ridiculous adventures in unfeasible vehicles, the chance to explore the Trail before it's lost forever was a personal challenge she couldn't ignore – yet it would sometimes be a terrifying journey.

Setting out from Hanoi on an ageing Honda Cub, she spent the next two months riding 2,000 miles through the mountains and jungles of Vietnam, Laos and Cambodia. Battling inhospitable terrain and multiple breakdowns, her experiences ranged from the touching to the hilarious, meeting former American fighter pilots, tribal chiefs, illegal loggers and bomb disposal experts.

The story of her brave journey is thrilling and poignant: a unique insight into a little known face of Southeast Asia.

'Utterly absorbing and impossible to put down.'

Jason Lewis

Have you enjoyed this book?
If so, why not write a review on your favourite website?

If you're interested in finding out more about our books,
find us on Facebook at **Summersdale Publishers** and follow
us on Twitter at **@Summersdale**.

Thanks very much for buying this Summersdale book.

www.summersdale.com